TEEN
SUICIDE

Other Books in the At Issue Series:

TEEN
SUICIDE

Tamara L. Roleff, *Book Editor*

David L. Bender, *Publisher*

Bruno Leone, *Executive Editor*

Bonnie Szumski, *Editorial Director*

David M. Haugen, *Managing Editor*

An Opposing Viewpoints® Series

Greenhaven Press, Inc.
San Diego, California

Library of Congress Cataloging-in-Publication Data

Teen suicide / Tamara L. Roleff, book editor.
    p.   cm. — (At issue)
    Includes bibliographical references and index.
    ISBN 0-7377-0327-X (pbk. : acid-free paper). —
ISBN 0-7377-0328-8 (lib. : acid-free paper)
    1. Teenagers—Suicidal behavior—United States. 2. Gay
teenagers—Suicidal behavior—United States. 3. Depression in
adolescence—United States. 4. Adolescent psychology—United
States. 5. Teenagers—United States—Social conditions. I. Roleff,
Tamara L., 1959–   . II. Series: At issue (San Diego, Calif.)

HV6546.T42   2000
362.28'083'0973—dc21   99-055610
                                                            CIP

©2000 by Greenhaven Press, Inc., PO Box 289009,
San Diego, CA 92198-9009

Printed in the U.S.A.

Table of Contents

Introduction

Adam Reule's classmates in Cottage Grove, Minnesota, wanted to include a full-page memorial in their 1998 yearbook dedicated to him and another student who had died before their graduation. Friends of Annette Sander and Jennifer Powell of Victorville, California, wanted to remember their deaths in 1995 by planting trees on the campus of the high school the two girls attended. Across the country, memorial gestures like these are controversial because they are dedicated to teens who died by committing suicide.

Memorials to suicide victims make some parents, school administrators, teachers, suicidologists, and others uneasy because they fear that memorializing suicide victims will promote suicide contagion, the potential that some teens may be influenced to commit suicide by someone else's suicidal behavior. For example, according to many of those who work with teens at risk, teens who feel unloved and unappreciated see suicide victims receiving massive amounts of attention through memorials and other outpourings of grief, and may be inspired to commit suicide so that they, too, can receive that type of attention. However, Jodi Brandenberger, a counselor with the San Bernardino County Office of Education, points out that these teens do not think the situation through:

> A child may think, "I'll never be the homecoming queen, but at least I can memorialize myself with a tree or be in a yearbook." And they think they'll somehow be able to hang around and see it for themselves.

Teens craving attention do not see the mistake in their logic: It is impossible for them to enjoy the attention when they are dead.

Other experts believe that memorials to suicide victims are not appropriate because they glamorize or condone suicide. They contend that teens who are considering suicide may perceive memorials to a suicide victim as society's way of honoring the suicidal behavior, rather than as a way of mourning the victim's death. Walt Lyszak, Adam Reule's high school principal, explains why he initially opposed a memorial page in the yearbook: "There is a possibility of kids feeling that they have become immortal by being in the yearbook." (The school eventually reached a compromise with the senior class; small portraits of Adam, who committed suicide, and the other student, who was killed by a drunk driver, were placed along with their names and the dates of their births and deaths on a full-page photo of a nature scene.) Pamela Cantor, a psychologist and lecturer at Harvard University, agrees that memorials can be dangerous and explains why suicide victims should not be memorialized:

> It gives the wrong message . . . that someone who should have used more constructive means to deal with their prob-

lems, such as therapy, took a destructive means—not only destroying themselves but their families and their circle of friends. This is something we should not memorialize, but pity. We should be grieving these kids, not eulogizing them.

According to Cantor and other suicidologists, memorializing teens who committed suicide may lead other troubled teens to think that suicide is an acceptable method of resolving their crises instead of trying to find alternative solutions to their problems.

Not all suicide experts and counselors agree that memorials for suicide victims should be banned. Some believe that memorials to suicide victims may actually prevent future suicides. Mark DeAntonio, an adolescent psychiatrist in Los Angeles, argues why suicide victims should be memorialized:

> People like to keep suicide secret because it is so disturbing, but silence doesn't resolve the issue. It just makes the suicide even more mysterious. A bench or a tree [dedicated to the student suicide victim] acknowledges that someone was lost—that we failed to protect an adolescent. And kids deal better with suicide when it's out in the open to discuss.

In DeAntonio's opinion, memorials present the perfect opportunity to discuss suicide prevention among other students.

Other mental health authorities maintain that a death by suicide should be treated no differently than any other death. Memorials for teen suicides are appropriate, argues David Shaffer, an expert on teen suicide and a psychiatrist at Columbia University in New York, because most teen suicides are the result of mental illness. "If we can feel sorry, plant a tree and pay our respects for a child who died of leukemia, why can't we do the same thing for a child who died of depression?" He contends that teens suffer a risk of greater emotional harm if suicides are ignored, rather than remembered for the lessons they can teach. Furthermore, suicide experts contend that arguments against "condoning" suicide by approving a memorial are misguided. Mary Kluesner, president of the Minneapolis-based organization Suicide Awareness-Voices of Education, asserts that inherent in the belief that memorials condone suicide

> is a disapproval and condemnation of the person who died of suicide. This is one of the modern punishments suffered by families whose loved one died from a brain disease.

By not remembering the suicide victim's death, she maintains, society is punishing the victim's family for a death that is not its fault.

Others contend that fears that memorials prompt suicide contagion are irrational. Kluesner maintains that acknowledging Adam Reule's or any other student's suicide with a memorial page in a yearbook does not encourage other teens to commit suicide:

> There are no documented scientific studies, only rumor and assumed belief, that contagion is a reality. Suicide contagion is very, very rare. The patterning and copying behavior of adolescents does not necessarily transfer to suicide. The student who said, "Why would anyone kill themselves be-

cause we remembered our friend with a memorial page?"
most likely had the most mature response to the situation.

Prohibiting or discouraging mourners to remember suicide victims with a
memorial because authorities are apprehensive of what might happen is
absurd, she maintains.

Most authorities on teen suicide agree that the greatest threat to suicide contagion or clusters is media coverage of suicides and suicide
memorial ceremonies, not the memorials themselves. Although the media have become more careful about how they report suicides, they have
been blamed for several teen suicide clusters in the late 1980s and early
1990s. Four teenagers in Bergenfield, New Jersey, killed themselves in
1987 in a suicide pact that involved carbon monoxide poisoning. Their
suicides received extensive media coverage, and a few days later, two
more teens killed themselves in a similar manner in Chicago. A third teen
killed himself a week later by carbon monoxide poisoning; investigators
found a clipping in his room about the Bergenfield suicides. Suicides by
teens using carbon monoxide were also reported the same week in Illi-
nois, Nebraska, and Washington. Likewise, the suicides of Annette Sander
and Jennifer Powell in 1995 generated widespread news coverage with
predictable results. Another teen in Victorville killed herself following the
report of the girls' suicides, and within the next seven months, sixteen
other teen girls attempted suicide.

Suicide experts agree that there is rarely one single reason to explain
why a person committed suicide. Suicide is usually the result of a complex set of factors that all contribute in one way or another to a person's
decision to commit suicide. Suicide memorials and contagion play just
one small part in the potential suicide victim's actions. *At Issue: Teen Suicide* examines some of the conditions that contribute to a person's decision to commit suicide, as well as the prevalence of teen suicide.

1

Teen Suicide Is a Serious Problem

Nancy Merritt

Nancy Merritt is with the Do It Now Foundation, an organization formed in 1968 to spread accurate information about drugs, alcohol, sexuality, and other behavioral health topics.

Teen suicide attempts and completions have risen steadily since the 1960s. Surveys have found that more than 25 percent of high school students and 10 percent of college students—a rate four times that of 1950—have seriously considered suicide. Suicidal teens generally fall into one of three groups: well-adjusted, but living in stressful conditions; depressed or anxious; or impulsive, aggressive, or self-destructive. Therefore, any teen who mentions committing suicide should be taken seriously.

To be or not to be?

It's a question that's thundered throughout history and one that pulses inside each of us, at one time or another in our lives.

Still, never has its pulse been more profound or its pull more compelling than for young people in America today.

Just consider some numbers. They're taken from recent surveys of college and high school students by the U.S. Centers for Disease Control:

• 27 percent of high-school students said they'd "thought seriously" about suicide in the past year; 8 percent said they'd actually tried to kill themselves.

• 10.3 percent of U.S. college students admitted serious thoughts of suicide; 6.7 percent had a suicide plan.

And today's teen-and-young-adult suicide epidemic isn't just a statistical blip, either, or a case of media hype.

The numbers of both suicide attempts and fatalities have risen steadily in the '90s, following similar jumps in the 1960s, '70s, and '80s.

Today, an estimated 276,000 kids between the ages of 14 and 17 try killing themselves each year, and more than 5,000 succeed. The current rate is four times that of 1950.

Reprinted from *Teen and Young Adult Suicide: Light and Shadows*, by Nancy Merritt, available at www.doitnow.org/pages/174.html, April 1998, with permission from the Do It Now Foundation.

The numbers are disturbing, and yet they only partially convey the tragedy of teen and young adult suicide, since every victim leaves a hole in the fabric of their communities and schools, and an ongoing ache in the hearts of their families and friends.

The epidemic is cause for concern—and for a new commitment to ending its spread. Because the real tragedy of youthful suicide is that it often can be prevented, if we know what to look for and care enough to act.

That's the point of this viewpoint.

Because stopping suicide starts with understanding the pain that suicidal people feel and helping them understand that they're not alone.

What types of people are more likely to attempt suicide?

At one time or another, just about everyone thinks of suicide. Still, young people who try to kill themselves usually fall into one of three main groups.

• *Well adjusted, but living with stressful situations.* They may be having difficulty in coping with a sudden crisis—their parents' divorce, for example, or the death of a friend. Failure in school, a romantic break-up, or any other major loss could also serve as a trigger.

• *Depressed or anxious.* People who feel stressed out or emotionally down are at a much higher risk of suicide. And the risk is higher still when emotional problems are coupled with substance abuse or interpersonal loss.

• *Impulsive, aggressive, or self-destructive.* Run-aways and drug and alcohol abusers often fit in this high-risk group. Teen suicide attempts are usually impulsive acts, and they're linked to impulsive kids.

Just consider some numbers. . . . 27 percent of high-school students said they'd "thought seriously" about suicide in the past year; 8 percent said they'd actually tried to kill themselves.

Other factors also play a role, and some have different impact than you might expect.

Take money, for example. Even though the problem is often portrayed in economic terms, suicide isn't usually a matter of dollars and cents. Statistics show that rich kids kill themselves as often as poor or middle-income kids.

On the other hand, gender does seem to be an important factor.

Many young people who are confused about their sexual identity—or who have experienced sexual guilt or embarrassment—can see suicide as a way to stop their shame or confusion.

And even though girls are about twice as likely to attempt suicide, boys are four times more likely to complete the act.

Is there a link between drugs and alcohol and suicide?

Yes, and not just those involving young people. Drugs and alcohol play a major role in suicides of all types.

Today, an estimated half of all suicides are committed by problem drinkers, while as many as two-thirds of all suicides involving young people center around drug use.

Even though girls are about twice as likely to attempt suicide, boys are four times more likely to complete the act.

Drugs and alcohol become particularly lethal when combined with emotional depression and interpersonal loss—a romantic break-up, for example, or the death of a loved one.

In fact, studies have shown that rates for suicide and attempted suicide are five to 20 times higher among drug and alcohol abusers than the general population.

Drugs and alcohol can be doubly dangerous since so few chemical abusers realize that depression is often drug-related. They think their feelings are a reflection of the way things really are, which can make them feel even more depressed—and more desperate.

Why do so many young people attempt suicide?

There are a lot of reasons for the current explosion of suicide among the young, but none is more important than the stress that kids go through today.

Because the fact is that growing up is more stressful today than it's ever been before.

A lot of factors have been blamed—everything almost from overpopulation and the breakdown of the family to increased pressure to excel and easy access to firearms. Still, we all know that the cumulative weight of life's stresses makes growing up a difficult experience for many young people, one that can seem overwhelming to some.

On top of everything else, there's the romantic image of suicide to contend with.

The fact that suicide is only messy and sad—and hardly romantic—doesn't seem to occur to many young people. It just seems a quick, easy way to make a point—or make someone sorry.

Then there's impulsiveness. Young people often act impulsively, and suicide is usually an impulsive act. Impulsiveness becomes a particular problem when someone is drunk or high.

A final reason kids commit suicide can be seen in the rash of "copycat" or cluster suicides that happen from time to time. Still, although they're highly publicized, cluster suicides only account for about 5 percent of all suicides.

Should all suicide threats be taken seriously?

Yes. Because so many young people are impulsive, threats of suicide should always be taken seriously. Suicide is one case where it's better to guess wrong about someone's intentions than to stay silent.

It's a myth that people who talk about suicide don't do it. They do. And you won't plant a seed in the person's mind that they wouldn't have planted themselves.

Suicidal people are stressed and depressed, not stupid. They're capable of thinking of suicide all by themselves.

So don't worry about putting ideas into their heads. If the ideas are there, they need to be talked about and dealt with. If they're not there, they won't take root simply because you mention them.

What are the warning signs?

Symptoms that may indicate whether or not a person is suicidal fall into three main groups:

• *Behavioral changes.* Warning signs can include changes in eating or sleeping patterns, withdrawal from friends and family, drinking or drug use, loss of interest in favorite activities, or giving away valued possessions.

• *Personality changes.* Common moods involve anger, anxiety, or depression. Other changes to look for include aggressiveness, hopelessness, hypersensitivity, boredom, difficulty concentrating, or an unexplained decline in school performance.

• *Health problems.* Red flags here could involve any serious or life-threatening illness, and even such "minor" complaints as frequent headaches, weight loss or gain, nausea, or fatigue.

At this point, we need to point out that the symptoms above don't necessarily mean someone is considering suicide.

Still, they are signs of a problem and need to be considered carefully.

Because the fact is that two-thirds of those who commit suicide give some warning first. That means it's up to us—as friends, teachers, parents, or relatives—to recognize the signal and respond, person to person.

Suicide solutions

If a person is really determined to die, he or she can usually figure out a way, no matter what anyone does. As painful as that may be, we need to accept it.

Still, many young people who consider—or even attempt—suicide aren't that determined to kill themselves. And there are a lot of things we can all do to make suicide more difficult and less likely.

Since about half of all young people who kill themselves do it with guns kept at home, one solution is for parents to keep guns hidden and unloaded, with bullets stored separately. Researchers say that suicidal impulses usually last only about 15 minutes. Making it past that time may be enough to defuse the situation.

The same rule applies to prescription drugs and alcohol. If you keep them in your home, keep them out of easy reach.

If you're a young person and a friend mentions suicide, talk to a caring adult—a parent, counselor, or someone else you can trust—as soon as you can. This is no time to keep a secret.

If you prevent your friend from committing suicide, he or she may be upset for a while. But chances are they won't be upset for long.

At least they'll have a lifetime to change their mind.

2

Suicide Rates Are Increasing Among Male Minority Teens

Fern Shen

Fern Shen is a staff writer for the Washington Post.

The suicide rates for African Americans, Native Americans, and Latino males is increasing dramatically compared to those of white males and females of all races. Researchers have yet to determine the cause for the rise. One theory holds that as minorities become absorbed into mainstream culture, they lose many of the family, religious, and cultural ties that may protect them against suicide. Others maintain that the increase in suicide rates is due to the social ills that disproportionately affect minorities, such as substance abuse and poverty. Public health officials need to concentrate on developing suicide prevention programs that are directed toward minority teen males.

S oaring suicide among America's young people set off alarms across the country in the last three decades, but social scientists are beginning to focus on especially sharp increases in suicide rates among one subgroup: young African American males.

From 1980 to 1993, suicide rates for black males ages 15 to 24 increased 63 percent, compared with 8 percent for white males in the same age group, according to an analysis of federal statistics. For all racial groups and both genders during that time period, suicide rates rose less than 10 percent in that age group.

A mystery

Why did young African American males, in the 1980s, begin taking their own lives at fast-growing rates?

It's an epidemiological mystery that dwells in the shadow of the only more rapidly rising killer of young black men, homicide, which accounted for 4,107 deaths in 1992 compared with 478 suicides. But it cries out for more attention than it has received, say many specialists who have tracked the statistics.

"With the sharp rise in homicides and everything else these children have to face, this is totally predictable. . . . We should have understood that suicide among young black men would follow," said Janice Hutchinson, medical director and acting administrator for the District's Children and Youth Services Administration.

But the causes and significance of this recent phenomenon remain a complex puzzle, one that researchers are just beginning to tackle.

Did the suicides of young black males in 1992, for example, occur more among those with limited education and low income? Or are the suicide deaths more rampant among those with better education and higher income, suggesting that as American blacks acquire greater social status, they acquire some of the majority white culture's problems as well? Preliminary research points in each of these conflicting directions.

Does the surge in suicide spring from social ills that simply afflict black Americans disproportionately, such as substance abuse and poverty? Or is there some deeper cultural disintegration among African Americans, as some have suggested, a fraying of the social ties that have helped them survive a history of oppression?

Then again, if there is a racial explanation for the phenomenon, how to explain the fact that suicide rates among young black females during this time period have remained static and even declined for some age groups?

Other researchers blame the easy availability of firearms for the climbing suicide rate, noting that almost all of the increase in suicides in the last decade involved guns.

From 1980 to 1993, suicide rates for black males ages 15 to 24 increased 63 percent, compared with 8 percent for white males in the same age group.

"The theories really bounce around. They run the gamut. You can find one that seems to explain it, but then along comes another piece of evidence that just doesn't fit," said Alex Crosby, an epidemiologist who tracks death rate demographics at the Centers for Disease Control and Prevention.

The trend is especially striking because it challenges an almost axiomatic belief in the African American community that blacks are not prone to suicide.

"We always said, 'Suicide is not our thing.' The black experience teaches you how to cope. It teaches you not to take suffering as a coincidence. It's a way of life," said the Rev. Cecil L. Murray, pastor of First African Methodist Episcopal Church of Los Angeles, one of many ministers, counselors and social workers who have been troubled by the trend. The overall rate of suicide in the United States has not changed much in the last half-century, but while rates have flattened or declined among adults, they have soared dramatically among young people. Since 1950, suicide rates have nearly quadrupled among 15- to 19-year-olds.

"It's disturbing. . . . Somehow, suicide is eking its way down through the younger ages," said Lloyd B. Potter, a CDC behavioral scientist.

For decades, white males have committed suicide in much larger numbers and at higher rates than black males, and they still do. Homicide deaths among young black males still vastly outnumber the group's suicide deaths.

But it is the rapidly widening racial disparity in young men's suicide rates that is striking. In the late 1980s and early 1990s, suicide rates for 15- to 24-year-old black males veered sharply upward. From 1980 to1993, the rate rose from 12.3 per 100,000 to 20.1, a 63 percent increase, according to the CDC. By comparison, the suicide rate for white males in the same age group was relatively flat in those years, going from 21.4 to 23.1, an increase of 8 percent.

The rising suicide rate among young black males grows out of broad social changes that cut across socioeconomic lines.

If those trends continue, "suicide rates for young African Americans will be exceeding those of whites within a year or two," Crosby said.

District officials, as well as those in Maryland and Virginia, report statistics that mirror the trend. D.C. Medical Examiner Joye M. Carter is so concerned about the problem that she is searching for patterns by reviewing suicides during the last five years.

"We've had young people hang themselves, shoot themselves, a few have flung themselves in front of trains . . . and out of windows," Carter said. "It's apparent that young black males are choosing suicide in growing numbers."

One explanation for the phenomenon may be "the surge in substance abuse among women," Hutchinson said.

"It used to be the mom was the tenacious one who held the family up," she said. "And now they're tired, burned out, frustrated . . . and they're leaving the family to fend for itself."

Consider the recent suicide attempt of a preteenager, described by his counselor at the D.C. Children and Youth Services Administration.

"His parents are separated. He was mandated to stay with one parent. He wanted to go with the other parent, but the other parent said she didn't want the kid," said the counselor, noting that both parents are crack cocaine users.

"The child tried to overdose on medications he had been taking for depression," said the counselor, who asked that his name not be used for fear it would compromise the child's confidentiality.

Although some specialists explain the recent increase as a consequence of familiar societal ills, others describe it as a byproduct of integration and the rising status of African Americans. As blacks become more absorbed into the majority-white culture, according to this argument, they lose the unique family, religious and cultural ties that may account for the fact that African American suicide rates consistently have been lower than those of white Americans.

Sherry Molock, a Howard University professor who directs the school's clinical psychology department and is studying suicide among students at predominantly black colleges, suggests that the rising suicide rate among young black males grows out of broad social changes that cut across socio-economic lines.

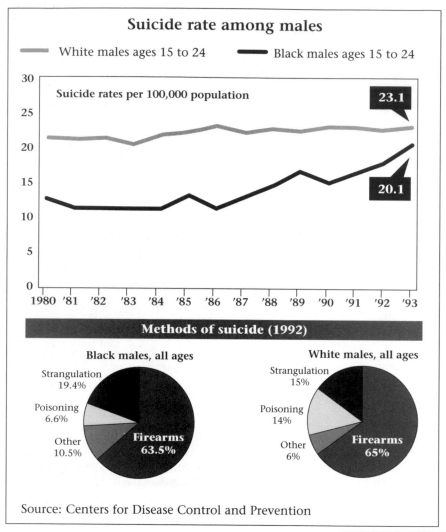

Suicide rate among males

——— White males ages 15 to 24   ━━━ Black males ages 15 to 24

Suicide rates per 100,000 population

23.1

20.1

1980 '81 '82 '83 '84 '85 '86 '87 '88 '89 '90 '91 '92 '93

Methods of suicide (1992)

Black males, all ages

Strangulation 19.4%
Poisoning 6.6%
Other 10.5%
Firearms 63.5%

White males, all ages

Strangulation 15%
Poisoning 14%
Other 6%
Firearms 65%

Source: Centers for Disease Control and Prevention

"Because we lived in a segregated society, we all lived together and had resources," Molock said, arguing that black families were more intact before integration, more likely to be exposed to church leaders and wage-earning professionals who were role models.

Not in dispute is the striking statistical evidence that suicide nation-wide is claiming young black males as never before. From 1980 to 1993:

• For males ages 10 to 14, the suicide rate increased 73 percent for whites but 358 percent for blacks.
• For males ages 15 to 19, the rate went up 23 percent for whites but 157 percent for blacks.

• For males ages 20 to 24, the rate fell 1.2 percent for whites but increased 30 percent for blacks.

African American males are just one of several groups that have exhibited troubling suicide trends in the last decade. Young American Indian males, for instance, continue to have some of the highest rates of suicide. The rate among 15- to 24-year-olds was 42 per 100,000 in 1992 and as high as 49 per 100,000 in 1990. Suicide rates for young Latino males appear to be rising faster than rates for whites, although not as fast as rates for African Americans, CDC officials said. They do not have firm statistics to go by, however, since many states, until 1989 or 1990, did not keep separate records of Latino suicides. In 1992, the rate for Latino males ages 15 to 24 was 16.3 per 100,000.

American Indians' high rates of alcoholism and depression, two factors associated with suicide, may partially account for their extremely high youth suicide rates, CDC officials said. Latino and American Indian youth are shouldering some of the same pressures—poverty, exposure to violence, weakened family ties—that could be driving up black male suicide rates.

The effects of socio-economic status

Researchers beginning to study the recent phenomenon of suicide among young blacks have explored the question of whether it is more pronounced among those with less education or lower income, a still murky matter when it comes to suicide generally. Early reports suggest the research is heading for conflicting conclusions.

One project, focusing on New York, New Jersey and Connecticut, has found that the parents of African American suicide victims were better educated and in a higher income bracket than the average for blacks in that area.

But David C. Clark, a professor of psychiatry and psychology at Chicago's Rush Presbyterian St. Luke's Medical Center, said the suicides among young black males he is studying in Chicago "are a bit skewed toward gang kids, more lower-income kids with conduct disorders."

A striking feature of the suicides among African American youths in Clark's study is that, in about 15 percent of the cases, the children killed themselves with guns in front of three or four friends. Those are the kinds of self-destructive acts that often are reported as "accidental shootings," according to some researchers, who said black suicide has been underreported. Suicide often is masked by labels such as "drug overdose" or by situations in which the victim purposely provokes a police officer or some other person to kill him.

Many studies have attributed the soaring suicide rate among young people in general to the growing proliferation of guns in American society, concluding that the availability of that more lethal method increases the likelihood that a suicide attempt will succeed. Indeed, the rate of attempted suicides has not increased in recent years, according to the few, limited surveys available.

According to the CDC, among 15- to 19-year-old black males, the rate of suicide committed with a gun quadrupled from 1980 to 1992, while suicide by other means among young black males generally declined. For further comparison, during the same period, among 15- to 19-year-old white males, firearm suicide rates increased 32 percent.

The surge in suicide should prompt public health officials, physicians, ministers and educators to establish prevention programs tailored to African Americans, said Alvin F. Poussaint, professor of psychiatry at Harvard University.

"The black community itself has been so focused on anti-violence programs, but somehow we've missed this," he said. "Consciousness has to be raised."

3

Homosexuality Is a Risk Factor for Teen Suicide

James Orlando

James Orlando wrote this viewpoint while attending Yale University.

Suicidal thoughts, attempts, and completions are much more common among gay teens than among straight teens, due to high levels of stress caused by society's intolerance of homosexuality and its harassment of gays and lesbians. This stress is further compounded by the fact that gay teens often feel unable to discuss their problems with friends, family, or counselors. Much of the pain, alienation, and suicidal thoughts experienced by gay teens could be alleviated if society accepted homosexuality and condemned the harassment of gays and lesbians.

S uicide among adolescents has been an increasingly distressing problem in our society. The number of teens who attempt suicide, as well as the number of teens who actually kill themselves, has risen substantially in recent years. Statistics show that teen suicides in the United States have doubled since 1960. Thankfully, the majority of suicide attempts are not successful: Every year over a quarter of a million adolescents in the United States attempt suicide, and about 2000 of these attempts are completed. Girls attempt suicide more often than do boys. Boys, however, are up to four times more likely to die from such attempts. This is due to the typical methods employed by boys versus girls in their attempts. Boys are more likely to use guns or other violent methods with a high chance of fatality; girls are more likely to overdose on medication or choose other methods with a greater chance of recovery.[1]

Suicide among homosexual teens

Even more disturbing are studies that show suicidal thoughts, intentions, and attempts among homosexual adolescents to be much more common than among heterosexual teens. For example, a recent survey of Massachusetts high school students found that 28.6% of straight students had seriously considered suicide within the previous year and 13.4% had

Reprinted from *Suicide and the Homosexual Adolescent*, by James Orlando, available at www.pantheon. cis.yale.edu/~jameso/. Reprinted with permission.

made at least one attempt within that year. By comparison, 41.7% of homosexual students had seriously considered suicide, and 27.5% had actually made an attempt.[2] Many of the motivations behind suicide attempts among both straight and gay teens are similar: family difficulties, identity issues, problems with peers or romantic partners, problems with substance abuse, etc. However, such problems are often more severe for youths who are homosexual. Moreover, teens who are questioning their sexuality, or who may have concluded firmly that they are homosexual, face a host of difficulties and obstacles which straight teens do not.

Suicidal thoughts, intentions, and attempts among homosexual adolescents . . . [are] much more common than among heterosexual teens.

Worse still, despite the great number of stressors which homosexual youths face on top of the typical turbulence of adolescence, gay and lesbian teens often feel less comfortable discussing their problems with friends, counselors, parents, or religious figures. A 1972 study published in the *Journal of the American Medical Association* (*JAMA*) asserted that the high rates of suicide attempts among young homosexual men indicated, in part, the isolation these young men feel in our homophobic society: "[T]he depth of revulsion toward homosexual activity in our society is such that there are very few places a young person can turn to discuss his problems without being condemned."[3] Our society has in many ways become more accepting of homosexuality in the years since that report was published. However, any progress that has been made does not change the reality that we still live in a society in which a great number of people, including people in powerful positions, still regard homosexuality to be a sin. News reports last year [1998] showed anti-gay protesters outside the memorial service for Matthew Shepard, the gay Wyoming college student who was brutalized and left for dead by two attackers. Clearly, we still do not live in a society in which it is safe or accepted to be homosexual. Such a hostile environment may prove especially harrowing for young men and women just coming to terms with their own sexuality.

The exact links between homosexuality and more frequent suicide attempts have not been established. Researchers and theorists often point to the trauma of coming out, the fear of rejection by parents and peers, and the impact of physical and verbal abuse as causal factors in the high rate of homosexual suicide. A study by Remafedi and colleagues (1991) seemed to indicate a link between sexual milestones for the homosexual adolescent and the onset of a suicide attempt. The researchers submitted surveys to 137 self-identified gay and bisexual youths, aged 14 to 21, from the Midwest and Northwest of the United States. Forty-one of the 137 individuals (30.0%) reported a past suicide attempt, including 18 reporting multiple attempts. Almost one third of the subjects reporting a suicide attempt made their first attempt in the same year that they identified themselves as bisexual or gay. The average age of the first homosexual experience for the 41 subjects who had attempted suicide was 14.38 years; the average age for non-attempters was 16.13. Attempters also reported coming out on average over a year earlier than non-attempters. The two groups differed on other variables predictive of suicidal behavior, including a history of sexual abuse (attempters were twice as likely to report an experience of sexual abuse than were non-attempters). Still, the researchers stressed the correlation between suicide attempts and milestones of homosexual self-identification, such as coming out or the first sexual experience with a same-sex partner.[4]

Studies of suicide among homosexual youth have often focused more on gay and bisexual males than on lesbian and bisexual females. This emphasis on males may reflect a common bias among male researchers to focus on male subjects, a bias which has eroded in recent years but still exists for many medical and psychological studies. This bias may also reflect a difference in the nature of homosexual male versus female teens' identification of themselves as homosexuals. The bias may also reflect the existence of wider community support networks for male versus female homosexuals, considering that many studies involve questionnaires submitted to self-identified homosexual teens, sometimes recruited through community organizations. One study which examined gender differences among bisexual and homosexual adolescents (Saewyc, 1998) did not find any significant differences on measures for emotional health, including suicidal thoughts or attempts, between male and female teen homosexuals. Among both male and female subjects over 15, [the percentage of] those reporting suicide attempts was slightly over 30%. One difference found was among those subjects 14 years old or younger. Among females in this younger group, 12.0% had attempted suicide. Among younger males, 22.4% had attempted suicide.[5] Several variables may account for this discrepancy. One possible factor is a younger age of identification as homosexual by the males than the females.

Researchers stressed the correlation between suicide attempts and milestones of homosexual self-identification, such as coming out or the first sexual experience with a same-sex partner.

Physical and verbal taunts, threats, and assault plague many homosexual adolescents, forcing all too many to hide their sexuality, sometimes even from themselves. The nature of such abuse can be relatively mild, but still significant, such as name-calling, or it may be as severe as physical or sexual assault. In 1994 Savin-Williams conducted a review of various other studies, attempting to establish a link between verbal and physical abuse of homosexual youths and various negative consequents, such as suicide. Savin-Williams admitted that many of the studies included in the review suffered from a very small sample size and may be non-representative of homosexual teens as a whole, considering that those youths who would participate in such studies are a self-selected group. Still, despite the unscientific nature of some of the research, such studies show some consistent patterns. Those students known to be gay do suffer from a great deal of physical and verbal abuse from peers, other adults, and even from parents. While such abuse is a source of great distress, the exact causal links between abuse and negative outcomes, such as suicide attempts, has not been established. The effects of such abuse may be greater on younger and non-white homosexual teens than upon older and white teens. Presumably, older and white homosexual teens may be better able to recognize and accept their homosexuality than are younger teens or teens from minority groups.[6]

Another study by Hershberger and D'Augelli (1995) attempted to establish a link between abuse, degree of family support and self-acceptance, and suicidality among homosexual teens. The researchers found that the strongest predictor of mental health was overall level of self-acceptance, which included acceptance of one's sexuality. The study also found that strong family support could help to moderate the deleterious effects of abuse, but only when such abuse was not severe. The researchers admitted that their study, like many such studies, was too heavily weighted towards male subjects, and that the self-selecting nature of their subjects leads to a questionable degree of representativeness. Moreover, the researchers urged the need for more longitudinal studies to examine the impact that physical and verbal abuse exerts on the long-term development of psychological well-being among homosexual individuals.[7]

An ideal society

In a better society, homosexuality would be accepted and harassment of homosexuals would be universally condemned. However, we are a long way from attaining such a society. The reality we face is that a large number of homosexual adolescents, tormented and alone, are attempting and committing suicide every year. Educators, researchers, and counselors must find a way to alleviate the pain and isolation that homosexual teens feel. Research indicates that even those persons trained to help alleviate psychological suffering may not be doing nearly enough. Kourany (1987) aimed to ascertain the prevalence of suicidal thinking among homosexual teens by administering a survey to a random sampling of psychiatrists specializing in the treatment of adolescents. However, when asked about their thoughts on suicidal gestures among homosexual teens, almost 60% of the psychiatrists reported having no experience or opinion on the subject. Many of the randomly drawn psychiatrists who chose to not answer the survey did so because they claimed to have no experience treating homosexual teens. The average participant in the study had been practicing psychiatry for over 18 years. It seems likely that many gay teens have not felt comfortable seeking counseling even when such help was needed, and that perhaps once in counseling, gay teens have not felt comfortable opening up about their sexuality.[8]

Clearly, many homosexual teens need somewhere to turn to discuss any number of issues, including many issues relating to their sexuality and the revelation of their sexuality to friends, school peers, and family. However, if these teens do not feel comfortable turning for help through traditional means, then either alternative means of support must be established, or the teens will have nowhere to turn. In a 1994 study Proctor and Groze offered a number of suggestions which could help to make homosexual adolescents feel less isolated. Schools could include gay- and lesbian-themed books within their libraries and include gay and lesbian households in the family living curriculum, to show gay and lesbian teens that they are not alone. However, both suggestions would face the opposition of conservative groups in many parts of the country. Additionally, peer counseling centers could be set up so that gay youths would feel free to discuss their problems with other gay youths. Youth centers and foster home programs should also be better sensitized to the needs of homosexual teens.[9]

It is the intolerance of our society, however, that creates the conditions which are truly killing these young men and women.

There are no easy solutions to the problem of suicide among adolescents, either gay or straight. The problem appears to be much more daunting, however, for homosexual teens. In a society which often condemns that which is different, sexual orientation seems to be the one realm, perhaps more than any other, where difference leads to open intolerance, harassment, and even abuse. Sadly, it should not be surprising that homosexual teens are more likely than straight teens to attempt and commit suicide. Adolescence is a difficult period of life, full of confusion, self-doubt, and questions about one's identity. When that identity includes the discovery of a "different" and berated sexual orientation, and when support systems for such teens are inadequate, the results, all too often, can only be disheartening. Many homosexual adolescents attempt to take their lives every year, and far too many succeed at doing so. It is the intolerance of our society, however, that creates the conditions which are truly killing these young men and women.

Notes

1. *Depression in Teens*. Taken off the website Depression.Com, 4-99. URL of this article: http://www.depression.com/special/special_01_teens.htm

2. Faulkner, A.H., and Cranston, K. (1998). Correlates of same-sex behavior in a random sample of Massachusetts high-school students. *American Journal of Public Health,* 88(2), 262–66.

3. Roesler, T., and Deisher, R.W. (1972). Youthful male homosexuality: Homosexual experience and the process of developing homosexual identity in males aged 16 to 22 years. *JAMA,* 219(8):1018–23.

4. Remafedi, Gary, Farrow, James A., and Deisher, Robert W. (1991). Risk factors for attempted suicide in gay and bisexual youth. *Pediatrics,* 87, 869–875.

5. Saewyc, E.M., Bearinger, L.H., Heinz, P.A., Blum, R.W., and Resnick, M.D. (1998). Gender differences in health and risk behaviors among bisexual and homosexual adolescents. *Journal of Adolescent Health,* 23(3), 181–8.

6. Savin-Williams, R.C. (1994). Verbal and physical abuse as stressors in the lives of lesbian, gay male, and bisexual youths: Associations with school problems, running away, substance abuse, prostitution, and suicide. *Journal of Consulting and Clinical Psychology,* 62(2), 261–9.

7. Hershberger, S.L., D'Augelli, A.R. (1995). The Impact of victimization on the mental health and suicidality of lesbian, gay, and bisexual youth. *Developmental Psychology,* 31(1), 65–74.

8. Kourany, R.F.C. (1987). Suicide among homosexual adolescents. *Journal of Homosexuality,* 13(4), 111–17.

9. Proctor, C.D., and Groze, V.K. (1994). Risk factors for suicide among gay, lesbian, and bisexual youths. *Social Work,* 39(5), 504–13.

4

The Availability of Guns in the Home Contributes to Teen Suicide

Educational Fund to End Handgun Violence and the Coalition to Stop Gun Violence

The Educational Fund to End Handgun Violence was founded in 1978 as an educational charity dedicated to ending gun violence. The Coalition to Stop Gun Violence is composed of forty-four civic, professional, and religious organizations and 120,000 individual members that advocate banning the sale and possession of all firearms.

Suicides in which a firearm is used account for nearly half the annual suicides in the United States. Using a gun to commit suicide almost always results in death, while other methods—such as poisoning—are not always lethal. Since teenagers are especially impulsive, they may believe the answer to their problems is suicide. If a gun is easily accessible, an impetuous teen has a much greater risk of committing suicide. Therefore, restricting the availability of guns will reduce the number of teen suicides.

Every year, firearm suicides account for just less than half of all firearm deaths and yet both sides of the gun control debate, along with the media and the general public, have shied away from this topic. It is time for the American people to understand that in looking for solutions to crime and violence by keeping a handgun at home they are placing themselves, and young people who often act impulsively, at much greater risk. More than 17,000 Americans die annually from self-inflicted firearm injuries. This staggering death toll would be greatly reduced if handguns were removed from homes.

Although firearm murders occupy the media spotlight, in reality, guns are used most frequently for self-destructive purposes. One study revealed that "[f]irearm suicides outnumbered firearm homicides in 40 of the 50 years between 1933 and 1982."[1] In 1992 (the last year for which

Reprinted, with permission, from "An Unspoken Tragedy: Firearm Suicide in the United States," a report by the Educational Fund to End Handgun Violence and the Coalition to Stop Gun Violence, May 31, 1995.

statistics are available) 37,776 Americans died as a result of firearm injuries. Of these firearm-related deaths, 18,169 (or 48 percent) were suicides, while 17,790 (or 47 percent) were homicides.[2] The remaining firearm deaths were caused by unintentional shootings.

In 1992, suicide was the ninth leading cause of death in the United States, accounting for the loss of 30,484 lives.[3] Almost 60 percent of these suicides were completed with guns. The same year 3,073 youths nationwide between 15 and 24 years old killed themselves with a gun.[4]

Statistics illustrate the extent of the problem of suicide in the United States. Nevertheless, the data are potentially misleading underestimates of actual figures due to under-reporting. One national team of researchers estimates that deaths resulting from suicide are attributed to other causes as much as 25–50 percent of the time.[5]

In the United States, white males, Native Americans, and the elderly experience the highest rates of suicide.[6] During the past four decades, however, rates among groups traditionally considered at low-risk of committing suicide increased dramatically. Firearm suicides account for most, if not all, of this growth.

Firearms as a method of suicide

Firearms are the most common means of suicide in the United States for both genders and all age groups.[7] Scientific studies reach varying conclusions regarding the use of handguns versus long guns in firearm suicides. It is often assumed that long guns are less likely than handguns to be used for suicide. However, Brent et al. (1991) reports that for his study sample the presence of rifles and shotguns presented as great a suicide risk as the presence of handguns. The researchers found that any gun in the home increases the risk of suicide.[8] Suicidal adolescents are 75 times more likely to commit suicide when a gun is kept in their home.[9]

Research indicates the suicide method that is most available and socially acceptable will be employed most often. In the United States, firearms meet both criteria. Thus, it is no surprise that guns are the most prevalent means of suicide.[10] A study comparing the regional rates of firearm prevalence and suicide found 3.0 per 100,000 persons increase in the suicide rate per 10 percent increase in the household prevalence of firearms.[11] If we hope to reduce the number of suicides committed in the United States we must simultaneously decrease or at least stabilize the number of guns in circulation and weaken the social conception that firearms pose little or no danger to owners and their families.

Suicide risk factors

Suicide is frequently considered a problem that solely affects the mentally ill. While certain psychiatric illnesses significantly predispose individuals to suicidal behavior, many other risk factors may prompt an individual's decision to end his or her own life.[12] Furthermore, while "mental illness is an important factor for suicide across all age groups, mental illness plays its least important role in the etiology of the suicide among youth ages 15–24, the group in which suicide rates have been increasing most rapidly."[13] Mental health and public health researchers have identified a wide variety of risk factors in suicide. These include the use of alcohol and illegal substances, living alone, and the lack of a high school education.[14]

Suicide attempts are also precipitated by "stressful life events [e.g., death of a loved one, loss of employment,] . . . loss or disruption of normal social support mechanisms [e.g., divorce, moving from one place to another, . . . and absent or inadequate social networks support."[15]

Young people appear to be particularly disposed to attempting suicide as the result of situational circumstances. Suicide attempts for this group frequently are motivated by a "shameful or humiliating experience such as an arrest, a perceived failure at school or work, or a rejection or interpersonal conflict with a romantic partner or parent."[16] One study (Hoberman and Garfinkel, 1988) found youths attempted suicide most frequently because of a fight with a parent, girlfriend or boyfriend, or because of problems in school.[17]

The recent rise in adolescent suicide rates is associated with increased alcohol and substance abuse in this age group. Brent et al. (1987) found a 46 percent increase between 1978 and 1983 in the proportion of youths committing suicide while intoxicated. While intoxicated, adolescents are more likely to employ firearms than any other means in a suicide attempt.[18]

The difficulty of screening suicide victims

It is extremely difficult, if not impossible, to identify all potential suicide victims. The motivation behind suicidal behavior is highly complex. Peterson et al. (1985) studied a group of suicide patients and found they "resemble[d] neither the 'average' drug overdoser nor the 'typical' completed suicide":

> The lack of suicide notes or other preparation and the fact that more than half the patients reported having had suicidal thoughts for less than 24 hours suggest a high degree of impulsivity. In spite of this, patients used highly lethal means in their self-destructive behavior.[19]

A careful look at the risks involved in suicide reveals that suicide can result from many factors other than mental illness, working either alone or in concert. Furthermore, suicide attempts are frequently unpredictable and typically impulsive.

Suicide used to be considered a problem largely limited to clinically depressed older white men. Since 1980, however, the majority of suicide victims in the United States has been forty years or younger.[20] Youths who actually attempt or complete suicide are a diverse class of individuals.[21] Young suicide victims typically are not depressed, but rather are experiencing problems at home or in school.[22] Furthermore, a distinct minority of youth suicide victims has been identified (Shaffer, 1988) who display no academic or behavioral problems whatsoever prior to their suicide attempt.[23]

Suicidal ideation and attempts are much more common in our society than many people realize. Many youths contemplate suicide at some point in their lives and almost 10 percent of all teens have reported attempting suicide.[24] One study (Smith and Crawford, 1986) found that 62.6 percent of a sample of high school students reported experiencing suicidal ideation or exhibiting suicidal behavior.[25]

Mental health professionals acknowledge the difficulties of screening suicide victims. One would imagine it is even more difficult for a member of the general public to objectively screen themselves or their family members. Furthermore, many of the risk factors to suicide that have been identified, such as divorce or job loss, cannot be predicted. Individuals should recognize that anyone—their spouse, their child, their parent, themselves—potentially could decide that life is not worth living. Even if the desire to die is instantaneous and fleeting, the likelihood that a suicide attempt will result in a fatality increases dramatically when firearms are present in the home.

Suicide attempts versus completions

Rosenberg et al. (1991) maintains "nonfatal assaults and suicide attempts may outnumber homicides and suicides by a ratio of more than 100 to 1."[26] O'Carroll et al. (1991) estimates "that there are approximately 25 suicide attempts for every completed suicide and that there are 750,000 adults who attempt suicide each year."[27] A study (Hopkins, et al., 1995) of fatal and non-fatal suicide attempts by adolescents in Oregon from 1988–1993 reported 31 nonfatal adolescent suicide attempts for every suicide fatality.[28] The study also revealed 75.5% of reported suicide attempts used drugs as the method of suicide. Yet, drug-related suicides represented 0.4% of the suicide fatalities. In comparison, firearm-related suicides accounted for 0.6% of total suicide attempts, but 78.2% of the suicide fatalities.[29]

The use of firearms has a high correlation to fatality. One study (Brent, et al., 1991) of suicide attempts and fatalities reported that 69% of the study sample died as a result of a firearm suicide. Whereas none of the surviving suicide victims used a gun in their attempt.[30]

Historically, males have completed suicide two[31] to five[32] times more often than females. Researchers maintain the historic discrepancy between male and female suicide fatality rates results from difference in choice of method. Males in fact attempt suicide much less often than females, but use highly lethal methods, such as inflicting firearm injuries or hanging, when they do. From 1988–1991, 65 percent of male suicide deaths resulted from firearms.[33] Females, on the other hand, attempt suicide an estimated two[34] to nine[35] times more frequently, but employ less lethal means, such as poisoning, that provide windows of opportunity for rescue and medical treatment.[36] Nevertheless, firearms are today the most common method used in female suicide fatalities.[37]

Suicidal adolescents are 75 times more likely to commit suicide when a gun is kept in their home.

Given the prevalence of suicide attempts compared to suicide completions it is evident that the lethality of the method involved is of critical importance. If the estimated 750,000 individuals attempting suicide each year were to do so with firearms, the national rate of suicide death would skyrocket. Not only are guns deadly because of their high degree of lethality in suicide attempts, but their increasing prevalence causes more suicide attempts. One study (Markush, 1984) predicts that if handgun prevalence were to reach 100 percent in the United States, the suicide rate would reach 42.6 per 100,000[38] (compared to the 1992 rate of 12.0 per 100,000).[39] In the interest of preventing such large numbers from ending their lives it is necessary to ensure that firearm access does not exceed its current rate.

The theory of method substitution

It has been proposed that suicidal individuals will find ways to kill themselves regardless of the availability of means. According to this hypothesis, if someone who wanted to die did not have access to a gun he or she would seek another method rather than abandoning his or her plans.

Several scientific studies have explored the issue of method substitution in suicide. One study investigated the cooking and heating gas in Birmingham, England, which once contained high levels of carbon monoxide and frequently was employed in suicide attempts. Between 1963 and 1970 this poisonous element was removed from the gas. Afterward, there was "a dramatic reduction in both unintentional and suicidal fatal carbon monoxide poisoning. Suicide incidence by other methods stayed almost the same. In other words, a common lethal agent was removed and use of others did not take its place."[40]

> *Not only are guns deadly because of their high degree of lethality in suicide attempts, but their increasing prevalence causes more suicide attempts.*

Another study (Loftin et al., 1991) investigated the impact of gun regulations on homicide and suicide rates in Washington, DC. In 1976, Washington, DC implemented a law prohibiting local residents from buying or selling handguns. Loftin found the regulation "was associated with a prompt decline in homicides and suicides by firearms in the District of Columbia. No such decline was observed for homicides or suicides in which guns were not used, and no decline was seen in adjacent metropolitan areas where restrictive licensing did not apply."[41]

Brent et al. (1991) maintains that youths would be less likely to substitute an alternative suicide method if guns were not easily accessed:

> [M]ethod substitution may be less likely to occur in adolescents and young adults, possibly because of the prominent role that impulsivity and substance abuse play in youthful suicide. The availability of a gun may play a more critical role in determining the lethality of a suicide attempt among impulsive youth than in older adults for whom suicide is a more premeditated act.[42]

Research on suicide method substitution remains inconclusive. However, it is possible that some suicide attempts may not occur if the means were difficult to obtain.[43] Regardless, the argument that suicidal individuals would substitute an alternative means for killing themselves if a gun were not available ultimately becomes moot when one considers the lethality of the method. The vast majority of firearm suicide attempts result in immediate fatalities. Suicide attempts by other means, such as ingestion of poison or exposure to high quantities of carbon monoxide, allow time for a change of heart and/or medical intervention. Thus, a decrease in availability of guns would save lives.

Association between high exposure to firearms and firearm suicide

The police comprise an occupational group with significant exposure and access to guns. Police in the United States experience unusually high overall and firearm and suicide rates:

> The suicide rate among [New York Police Department's] 31,000 is about 2.5 times higher than that of the general population. In (the past) 10 years, the NYPD suicide toll is 64 versus 20 killed in the line of duty. National statistics on police suicides are hard to find. But experts say the rate is two to three times higher than the general population.[44]

Another study analyzing suicide rates among policemen in New York City found that between 1934 and 1939 the Department's overall suicide rate far exceeded that of the city's civilian population at 84.5 per 100,000 versus 15.2 per 100,000. Furthermore, the study determined 9 out of every 10 suicide victims in the study group shot themselves with a revolver.[45]

Several unique characteristics of this sample pool preclude drawing a close analogy between the suicidal behavior of police and the national population. Nevertheless, the phenomenon is significant in terms of the lesson it provides regarding the ready availability of firearms to individuals who are familiar, and presumably somewhat comfortable, with such weapons. Experts agree that the unusually high rates of police suicide may be explained in part by easy access to a highly lethal instrument.[46] We propose an additional possible explanation. While pro-gun groups argue that properly trained individuals are immune from the risks associated with gun ownership, we maintain that individuals who are at ease with firearms may be more likely to use them for self-destructive purposes.

The impact of firearm access and availability on suicides

The choice of suicide method stems from the method's availability. Brent et al. (1991) analyzed adolescent suicides and found that most of the suicide victims who lived in a home that kept a gun chose to kill themselves with a gunshot, while suicide victims who lived in homes without guns rarely chose guns as an instrument of death.[47] It also has been reported that suicidal adolescents are 75 times more likely to commit suicide when a gun is present in the home.[48] Consequently, public health officials list increased gun control measures and reduced access to lethal weapons as the primary means of suicide prevention.[49]

People frequently purchase firearms in the interest of self-protection. However, research indicates a gun in the home is about 43 times more likely to be used for suicide or murder than self-defense.[50] Furthermore, firearms are rarely purchased immediately prior to suicide attempt. Rather, firearm suicides are overwhelmingly committed with guns that have been owned for some time.[51] Research indicates a mere 10 percent of firearm suicides result from firearms intentionally purchased for a suicide attempt.[52] Therefore waiting periods are of little value in reducing firearm suicide.

It has been suggested that the proper storage of firearms will circumvent the risks associated with keeping a gun at home. Experts have explored this proposal. Kellermann et al. (1992) found that "[h]ouseholds with guns kept in an unlocked place were associated with a higher risk of suicide than households in which guns were kept in a locked place. . . . [Nevertheless,] homes with guns of any sort were associated with a significantly higher risk of suicide than homes without guns, regardless of the type of gun or the method of storage."[53] Brent et al. (1991) found "no difference in the methods of storage of firearms among the [suicide victims, attempters, and psychiatric controls in his study], so that even guns stored locked, or separate from ammunition, were associated with suicide by firearms."[54] Brent concluded, "[t]he availability of guns in the home, independent of firearm type or method of storage, appears to increase the risk for suicide."[55]

Youths would be less likely to substitute an alternative suicide method if guns were not easily accessed.

In theory, one would expect that firearm owners would store their guns properly if they received education on the subject. Hemenway et al. (1995) studied this possibility and found that people trained in proper firearm storage techniques actually are much more likely to have a gun at home that is unsafely stored (i.e., both loaded and unlocked).[56] While no conclusions have been reached as to why this is, one may hypothesize that firearm training gives some owners a false sense of security in their knowledge and skill that may lead to recklessness. Hemenway et al. concluded that his research "cast doubt on whether firearm training, at least as currently provided, will substantially reduce the inappropriate storage of firearms."[57]

While proper storage of guns in the home (i.e., unloaded, securely locked, and kept separately from ammunition) is preferable to improper storage (i.e., loaded and kept in a dresser drawer, under a pillow, on a closet shelf, etc.) research indicates that it makes little or no difference in the likelihood of guns in the home being used in a suicide attempt.[58] Blumenthal et al. (1990) reports that "[t]he availability of firearms appears to be a more significant risk factor than the accessibility, so that storage of the gun in a more 'secure' fashion is probably not as protective as simply removing the gun from the home environment."[59] Consequently, we advocate firearms be removed or remain absent from homes.

Access to firearms a risk factor to suicide

Mental health and public health researchers consider easy access to firearms a significant and independent risk factor to suicide.[60] Kellermann et al. (1986) found suicides account for the majority of firearm deaths occurring within the confines of a private home: "For every case of self-protective homicide involving a firearm kept in the home, there were 1.3 accidental deaths, 4.6 criminal homicides, and 37 suicides involving firearms."[61] In a later study Kellermann et al. (1992) concluded "the presence of guns in the home was associated with an increased risk of suicide among women as well as men, across all age strata, and among whites."[62]

Historical trends in firearm suicide

The national rate of suicide for all ages in aggregate rose somewhat steadily from a low point of approximately 10 per 100,000 in 1943 to a high point of 13 per 100,000 in 1986.[63] Since then, the rate has leveled off. In 1992, the national rate for all ages combined was 12.0.[64] Baker et al. (1992) reports that between 1968 and 1986, the firearm suicide rate "increased by 36 percent, while suicide by all other means combined remained virtually unchanged."[65]

In the past, the overwhelming majority of suicide victims in the United States were older white males. During the last few decades, however, suicide rates have increased among new demographic groups including females and adolescents:

> Although the rate of suicide remains highest among older white males, rates of suicide have grown disproportionately in groups that were traditionally at low risk, and increasing rates of firearm suicide appear to be striking part of this dynamic transformation. Between 1960 and 1980 the total number of females committing suicide by all means other than firearms increased 16 percent, while the number of females committing suicide using firearms more than doubled. Suicide of young persons ages 5–19 by all means other than firearms increased 175 percent between 1960 and 1980; over the same period the percentage increase of suicide by firearms among this age group was 299 percent. Nonwhites, typically a low-risk group for suicide, experienced an 88 percent increase in non-firearm suicides between 1960 and 1980, compared with a 160 percent increase in the volume of firearm suicide.[66]

A lack of data precludes drawing a causal link between an increase in gun availability and an increase in firearm suicide rates. Nevertheless, research reveals the two trends clearly are associated.

In the 1960s and 1970s the number of firearms circulating throughout the United States sky-rocketed with the tripling of firearm imports and domestic production during this period.[67] The Bureau of Alcohol, Tobacco and Firearms released a report that estimated 54 million firearms in circulation in the United States in 1950; 104 million in 1970; and over 200 million in 1989.[68] In the six years since, domestic producers have poured out approximately 3.5 million guns annually,[69] while importers have contributed another half million each year.[70] Researchers estimate that in 1968 there were 50 guns per 100 civilians. In contrast, by 1979, there were approximately 75 guns per 100 civilians.[71] Numerous polls indicate about 50 percent of Americans admit to having a gun at home. Today there are approximately 220 million guns in the U.S. which equals all the adults and more than half the children in America.[72]

This noteworthy increase in firearm ownership corresponds to a drastic jump in firearm suicide rates. Whereas firearms were responsible for 47 percent of all suicides in 1960, they were responsible for 56 percent of all suicides by 1977[73] and 61% by 1990.[74] One researcher noted that "[v]irtually all of the increase [in suicide rates] since 1963 has been in suicide by firearms."[75]

Youth suicide rates

In the United States the highest suicide rates occur among the elderly. While the nation's overall suicide rate appears to have reached a plateau, youth suicide rates continue to climb, marking a distinct and alarming shift in suicides to the youngest age groups.[76] Youths also have experienced a rise in firearm suicide rates greater than any other age group in the country.[77]

Prior to 1955 the suicide rate for youths aged 15- to 24-years in the United States remained constant at a much lower point than the national rate for all ages combined. Starting in the mid-1950s, however, the suicide rate among this age group began to increase significantly.[78] In 1950, the suicide rate for persons 15- to 24-years of age was 4.5 per 100,000. By 1980, the suicide rate for the same age group had increased more than 300 percent to over 12.0 per 100,000.[79] In 1992, the suicide rate for 15- to 19-year-olds was still higher at 13.0 per 100,000, and exceeded the national rate for all ages combined of 12.0 per 100,000.[80]

In an effort to address the escalating problem of youth suicide, the U.S. Department of Health and Human Services in 1979 set a public health goal to lower the suicide rate for 15- to 24-year-olds from the 1978 rate of 12.4 per 100,000 to less than 11.0 per 100,000 by 1990.[81] In 1992, however, this goal still had not been reached, and the suicide rate for this age group in fact had worsened further.[82]

Research indicates a gun in the home is about 43 times more likely to be used for suicide or murder than self-defense.

The self-destructive use of guns is the most common method of suicide for young people in the United States.[83] Guns are largely, if not entirely, responsible for the dramatic increase in suicide rates for the nation's youths.[84] Since 1970, firearm suicide has risen three times more quickly than suicide by other means among 15- to 19-year-olds, and ten times more quickly among 20- to 24-year-olds.[85] During the years 1980–1992, the suicide rate for persons 15- to 19-years of age increased 28.3%, of which firearm-related suicides account for 81%.[86] Today, approximately 60 percent of all teenagers in the United States who complete a suicide do so with guns.[87]

Data indicate that even younger children are falling victim to the same phenomenon. Both the firearm-related and the overall suicide rate has increased for 10- to 14-year-olds in the United States. For the years

1980–1992, the suicide rate for young people aged 10 to 14 increased 120% overall.[88] Firearms are now the most frequent method of suicide for males as well as females within this age group.[89]

Youth exposure to firearms

Youths in the United States today have greater exposure and access to guns. A survey conducted by the Harvard School of Public Health in 1993 reported startling findings regarding the ease with which youths today can obtain guns:

> A substantial 59 percent majority of all young people aged 10–19 in school today say they "could get a handgun if I wanted one." In the central cities 63 percent say they could get one, as do 58 percent of those in the suburbs, and 56 percent in small towns and rural areas.[90]

> Two in three who know where to get a handgun say they could get one within a 24 hour period. A higher proportion of young people who go to private and parochial schools say they know how to get a gun than do those who go to public schools.[91]

Nationally, one out of two households admits to possessing firearms.[92] In homes where there is both a child and a gun, odds are the gun is stored dangerously—accessible and loaded. Among parents who admit to having a gun in their home, 59% also admit that their firearm is not locked away from their children.[93]

Guns are largely, if not entirely, responsible for the dramatic increase in suicide rates for the nation's youths.

It is possible that the gun culture surrounding youths contributes to the rampant increase in youth firearm suicide in recent decades. As youths gain greater access in our increasingly gun-saturated society, it is more likely that they will employ a gun as a means of suicide.

The role of impulse in youth suicide

The decision to end one's life is frequently sudden, uncalculated, and fleeting. It is that much more so for adolescents. Firearms are one of the most lethal means of suicide available. Easy access to highly lethal methods significantly increases the likelihood of an impulsive suicide attempt resulting in death. Whereas other methods, such as drug overdoses, allow time for medical intervention, firearms usually produce instant fatalities. Nevertheless, firearms are widely prevalent in homes throughout the United States. Consequently, young people—a group particularly prone to impulsive acts—often have little difficulty locating a gun at home leading to a lethal suicide attempt that was far from premeditated or sincere.

Researchers have determined that youths who attempt suicide rarely have a "clear and sustained"[94] desire to die. One study of adolescent attempters found two-thirds did not in fact have any desire to die.[95] Instead, youth suicide attempts frequently constitute highly impulsive efforts to communicate strong emotions or a cry for help.[96] Access to firearms under such circumstances is very problematic as guns are associated with such a high degree of lethality providing little opportunity for second thoughts or outside intervention.

Female suicide rates

In the United States both males and females commit suicide most frequently by shooting themselves. While firearm suicide among males is an on-going and growing problem, its prevalence among females is a relatively new phenomenon.[97]

Both the overall and firearm suicide rates for American females peaked between 1970 and 1977.[98] However, the proportion of women choosing guns as a method of suicide increased since the mid-1950s.[99] In 1970, 30 percent of all female suicides in the United States were attributed to firearms. By 1989, 41 percent of all female suicides were firearm-related.[100]

One researcher (Weed, 1985) reported that in 1960 females completed suicides most frequently by poisoning themselves. That year only 25.3 percent of all female suicides resulted from firearms injuries. By 1982, however, females completed suicides most often by shooting themselves and guns were responsible for 40.7 percent of all female suicides. That same year guns were responsible for 64.2 percent of all male suicides. Thus, while firearm suicides still are attributed disproportionately to males, the gap between female and male firearm suicide rates rapidly is narrowing.[101]

The trend of increased firearm use in female suicides is particularly evident among younger age groups.[102] In 1970, according to one study, firearms were responsible for 32.3 percent of suicides committed by females between 15 and 24 years old. In 1984, firearm-related deaths accounted for 51.3 percent of suicides committed by the same demographic group.[103]

In the past, men and women in the United States favored different methods of committing suicide. Males traditionally utilize firearms, while women utilize less lethal means such as poison. While this still is true, an increasing percentage of females end their lives by fatally shooting themselves. The trend of increasing use of firearms in female suicide is particularly alarming given that females attempt suicide much more frequently than males and that firearm suicides carry a greater fatality rate than other methods traditionally used by women. Since females attempt suicide so frequently, any increase in use of firearms will result in a dramatic increase in female suicide fatalities.

Female exposure to firearms

A marked slump in gun sales in the United States during the early 1980s, attributed to saturation of the traditional white male market, prompted the firearms industry to cultivate a pool of new customers among a large and previously untapped market—women.[104]

Glick (1994) conducted a study on the targeting of women by firearms manufacturers and distributors and noted its association to the increased use of guns in female suicide:

> With the increased marketing of firearms—specifically handguns—to women for self-defense, female patterns of suicide have changed. . . . In 1970, poisoning was the suicide method most commonly used by women. This method has decreased in inverse proportion to firearm use. Now, like men, women most often kill themselves with firearms.[105]

Through various advertising techniques the gun industry exploits women's fear of victimization and touts firearms as a protective device that will bring them less harm and more good. Again, heightened exposure and access to firearms results in a heightened possibility of their use in suicide attempts.

The societal cost of firearm suicide

Many people assume a stranger's suicide will have no impact on their lives, but rather only will affect the individual victim and the victim's survivors. On the contrary, suicides burden our society with economic costs, the loss of potential life, and the emotional trauma inflicted on the family and friends of suicide victims.

Years-per-life-lost, assuming the average life expectancy in the United States is 65 years, (YPLL-65) is a formula used by statisticians to calculate the years of potential life our society loses when younger individuals die a premature death. The formula captures the significance of the fact that certain agents of death tend to result in the loss of younger lives. The Center for Disease Control (CDC) reported a significant increase in YPPL-65 due to firearm injuries between 1980 and 1991. The increase in YPPL-65 was greater for firearm homicides than firearm suicides, as firearm homicide victims were frequently younger than firearm suicide victims. Between 1980 and 1991 firearm suicides increased 20.3 percent. YPLL-65 attributed to suicide rose 14.7 percent, and firearm suicides were responsible for nearly 80 percent of this rise.[106]

While firearm suicides still are attributed disproportionately to males, the gap between female and male firearm suicide rates rapidly is narrowing.

CDC researchers concluded "[i]f present trends continue, firearm-related injuries will become the leading cause of injury-related mortality in the United States during the next ten years."[107] This prediction is quickly being realized. According to Wintemute (1995) statistical trends indicate "firearm violence is outpacing motor vehicle injuries as the leading cause of traumatic death in this country."[108]

In an earlier study (1992) Wintemute analyzed the economic costs of firearm violence in the United States. His study mentions a report written by the United States General Accounting Office which "estimated a cumulative lifetime cost of \$14.4 billion for firearm injuries sustained in

1985, of which $863 million are expenses for direct medical care."[109] In 1989 researchers estimated the annual health care costs for suicide attempters alone to be approximately $116.4 million.[110]

Health care costs for survivors of firearm suicide attempts can run extremely high, especially compared to health care costs for suicide survivors who employ less destructive means in their attempts. Obviously pumping an individual's stomach after they swallowed a bottle of aspirin requires less treatment and expertise than operating on an individual who shot themselves. Wintemute (1992) reports the illustrative case history of an 18-year-old male who tried to kill himself "by shooting himself in the head with a .22-caliber handgun" and survived[111]:

> He underwent [two operations] . . . was intubated for 4 weeks, and developed [serious complications]. . . . The patient was discharged home after 54 days. Initial hospital charges: $103,771; $103,601 reimbursed by private insurance, $170 bad debt. The patient was readmitted 20 times for tracheal dilation procedures and has had similar procedures performed as an out-patient. The first 10 in-patient readmissions, like the initial hospitalization, were paid for largely by the patient's health insurance. In 1986 he lost his insurance coverage, and the final 10 admissions were paid for entirely by public funds. Subsequent hospital charges (in-patient care only): $95,000; $52,338 reimbursed by private insurance, $8,160 reimbursed by Medicaid, $34,502 bad debt.[112]

Preventing people from utilizing firearms in suicide attempts by eliminating or minimizing access to firearms would help individuals by reducing the risk of successful suicide attempts, and help the public at-large by reducing the fiscal burden of certain medical costs and increasing the years of potential life contributed to our society.

We propose a two-pronged approach to the problem of firearm suicide. We must reduce both the demand and the supply of guns in this country.

Public education campaigns must inform the public about the dangers of firearm ownership. We must reveal the fallacy of "protecting" one's family with a gun in the home. People must learn that a gun in the home puts themselves and their family at risk. We also must de-glamorize guns and offer youth opportunities to make positive contributions to their community.

Regulation of firearms and enforcement of existing laws must be increased in order to cap, if not reduce, the number of guns in circulation and thereby decrease access to one of the most lethal methods of suicide. Most importantly, individuals must acknowledge the risks associated with firearm ownership and remove and/or ban guns from their homes.

Notes

1. Garen J. Wintemute, MD, MPH, Stephen P. Teret, JD, MPH, Jess F. Kraus, MPH, PhD, and Mona Wright, BS, "The Choice of Weapons in Firearm Suicides," *American Journal of Public Health*, July 1988, Vol. 78, No. 7, p. 824.

2. Kenneth D. Kochanek, MA, and Bettie L. Hudson, "Advance Report of Final Mortality Statistics, 1992," *Monthly Vital Statistics Report*, December 8, 1994, Vol. 43, No. 6, Supplement, pp. 9, 56.

3. Kochanek and Hudson, pp. 2, 36.

4. Kochanek and Hudson, p. 56.

5. National Center for Injury Prevention and Control, "Injury Prevention: Meeting the Challenge," *American Journal of Preventive Medicine*, New York, NY: Oxford Press, 1989, Vol. 5, No. 3, p. 252.

6. Mark L. Rosenberg and M.A. Fenley (Eds.), *Violence in America: A Public Health Approach*, New York, NY: Oxford University Press, 1991, p. 7.

7. Rosenberg and Fenley, p. 7, and Susan P. Baker, Brian O'Neill, Marvin J. Ginsburg, and Guohua Li, *The Injury Prevention Notebook*, Second Edition, 1992, p. 66.

8. David A. Brent, MD, Joshua A. Perper, MD, LLB, MSc, Christopher J. Allman, Grace M. Moritz, ACSE, Mary E. Wartella, MSE, Janice P. Zelenak, PhD, "The Presence and Accessibility of Firearms in the Homes of Adolescent Suicides, A Case Control Study," *Journal of the American Medical Association*, December 12, 1991, Vol. 266, No. 21, p. 2989.

9. Mark L. Rosenberg, MD, James A. Mercy, PhD, Vernon N. Houk, MD, "Guns and Adolescent Suicides," (Editorial) *Journal of the American Medical Association*, December 4, 1991, Vol. 226, No. 21, p. 3030.

10. National Center for Injury Prevention and Control, "Injury Prevention: Meeting the Challenge," p. 255, and Robert E. Markush, MD, MPH, and Alfred A. Bartolucci, PhD, "Firearms and Suicide in the United States," *American Journal of Public Health*, February 1984, Vol. 74, No. 2, pp. 17, 20.

11. Markush and Bartolucci, p. 10.

12. Rosenberg and Fenley, pp. 188, 192.

13. Rosenberg and Fenley, p. 193.

14. Arthur L. Kellermann, MD, MPH, Frederick P. Rivera, MD, MPH, Grant Somes, PhD, Donald T. Reay, MD, Jerry Francisco, MD, Joyce Gillentine Banton, MS, Janice Prodzinski, BA, Corrine Fligner, MD and Bela B. Hackman, MD, "Suicide in the Home in Relation to Gun Ownership," *New England Journal of Medicine*, Vol. 327, No. 7, August 13, 1992, p. 470.

15. Rosenberg and Fenley, p. 190.

16. Ann F. Garland and Edward Zigler, "Adolescent Suicide Prevention: Current Research and Social Policy Implications," *American Psychologist*, February 1993, p. 173.

17. Garland and Zigler, pp. 173–4.

18. Garland and Zigler, p. 173.

19. Linda G. Peterson, MD, McKim Peterson, MD, Gregory J. O'Shanick, MD, and Alan Swann, "Self-Inflicted Gunshot Wounds: Lethality of Method Versus Intent," *American Journal of Psychiatry*, February 1985, Vol. 142, No. 2, p. 230.

20. Rosenberg and Fenley, p. 4.

21. Garland and Zigler, p. 172.

22. Rosenberg and Fenley, p. 4.

23. Garland and Zigler, p. 172.

24. Garland and Zigler, p. 174.

25. Garland and Zigler, p. 170.

26. Rosenberg and Fenley, p. 3.

27. Rosenberg and Fenley, p. 184.

28. DD Hopkins, MS, JA Grant-Worley, MS, DW Fleming, MD, State Epidemiologist, State Health Division, Oregon Department of Human Resources, National Center for Injury Prevention and Control, Centers for Disease Control and Prevention, "Fatal and Nonfatal Suicide Attempts Among Adolescents—Oregon, 1988–1993," *Morbidity and Mortality Weekly Report*, April 28, 1995, Vol. 44, No. 16, p. 321.

29. Hopkins, et al., p. 315.

30. Brent et al., p. 2992.

31. Peterson, et al., p. 230.

32. Rosenberg and Fenley, p. 186.

33. National Center for Health Statistics.

34. Peterson, et al., p. 230.

35. Susan J. Blumenthal, MD, MPA, and David J. Kupfer, MD (Eds.), *Suicide Over the Life Cycle: Risk Factors, Assessment, and Treatment of Suicidal Patients,* Washington, DC: American Psychiatric Press, 1990, p. 261.

36. Garland and Zigler, p. 170, and Rosenberg and Fenley, p. 186.

37. Rosenberg and Fenley, p. 186.

38. Markush and Bartolucci, p. 10.

39. Kochanek and Hudson, p. 5.

40. Susan P. Baker, MPH, "28,000 Gun Deaths A Year: What Is Our Role?" (Editorial), *Journal of Trauma,* 1976, Vol. 16, No. 6, p. 510.

41. Colin Loftin, PhD, David McDowall, PhD, Brian Wiersema, and Talbert J. Cottey, MS, "Effects of Restrictive Licensing of Handguns on Homicide and Suicide in the District of Columbia," *New England Journal of Medicine,* December 3, 1991, Vol. 325, No. 23, p. 1615.

42. Brent, et al., p. 2994.

43. Rosenberg and Fenley, p. 190.

44. John Ritter, "For Cops, A Deadly Combination," *USA Today,* December 28, 1994.

45. Markush and Bartolucci, pp. 18–19.

46. Jean Seligmann, Douglas Holt, Dante Chinni, and Elizabeth Roberts, "Cops Who Kill—Themselves," *Newsweek,* September 26, 1994, and Ritter, "For Cops, A Deadly Combination."

47. Brent, et al., p. 2992.

48. Rosenberg, Mercy, and Houk, p. 3030.

49. Blumenthal and Kupfer, pp. 266, 719, and Rosenberg and Fenley, p. 186.

50. Arthur L. Kellermann, MD, MPH, and Donald T. Reay, MD, "Protection or Peril? An Analysis of Firearm-Related Deaths in the Home," *New England Journal of Medicine,* June 12, 1986, Vol. 314, No. 24.

51. National Center for Injury Prevention and Control, "Injury Prevention: Meeting the Challenge," p. 255, and Kellermann, et al., "Suicide In the Home In Relation to Gun Ownership."

52. Susan Glick, MHS, *Female Persuasion: A Study of How the Firearms Industry Markets to Women and the Reality of Women and Guns,* Washington, DC: Violence Policy Resource Center, 1994, p. 41.

53. Kellermann, et al., "Suicide In the Home In Relation to Gun Ownership," p. 470.

54. Brent, et al., p. 2989.

55. Brent, et al., p. 2989.

56. David Hemenway, PhD, Sara J. Solnick, MS, Deborah R. Azrael, MS, "Firearm Training and Storage," *Journal of the American Medical Association,* January 4, 1995, Vol. 273, No. 1, p. 48.

57. Hemenway, et al., p. 46.

58. Blumenthal and Kupfer, and Brent, et al.

59. Blumenthal and Kupfer, p. 278.

60. Rosenberg and Fenley, p. 190.

61. Kellermann, et al., "Protection or Peril? An Analysis of Firearm-Related Deaths in the Home," p. 1557.

62. Kellermann, et al., "Suicide In the Home In Relation to Gun Ownership," p. 470.

63. Baker, O'Neill, Ginsburg, and Li, pp. 74–5.

64. Kochanek and Hudson, p. 5.

65. Baker, O'Neill, Ginsburg, and Li, p. 75.

66. Frank Zimring, "Policy Research on Firearms and Violence," *Health Affairs*, Winter 1993, Vol. 12, No. 4, pp. 114–5.

67. Markush and Bartolucci, p. 16.

68. Michael Isikoff, "200 Million Guns Reported in Circulation Nationwide," *Washington Post*, May 24, 1991.

69. Bureau of Alcohol, Tobacco and Firearms (BATF), June 29, 1994, "U.S. Firearms Production," *American Firearms Industry*, March, 1994, p. 41, and "U.S. Firearms Production 1993," *American Firearms Industry*, January, 1995, p. 74.

70. BATF, February 23, 1993.

71. Eve K. Moscicki, Jeffrey H. Boyd, "Epidemiologic Trends in Firearm Suicides among Adolescents," *Pediatrician*, 1985, Vol. 12, p. 56.

72. "Guns by the Numbers," *USA Today*, December 29, 1993, p. 3A., Isikoff, "200 Million Guns Reported in Circulation Nationwide," BATF, February 23, 1993, BATF, June 29, 1994, "U.S. Firearms Production," p. 41, and "U.S. Firearms Production 1993," p. 74.

73. Zimring, p. 114.

74. National Center for Health Statistics.

75. National Center for Injury Prevention and Control, "Injury Prevention: Meeting the Challenge," p. 253.

76. Moscicki and Boyd, "Epidemiologic Trends in Firearm Suicides among Adolescents," p. 52, James A. Weed, PhD, "Suicide in the United States: 1958–1982," Chapter 6 in *Mental Health United States*, Rockville, MD: NIMH, 1985, p. 135, Rosenberg and Fenley, p. 186, and Garland and Zigler, p. 169.

77. Moscicki and Boyd, "Epidemiologic Trends in Firearm Suicides among Adolescents," p. 52.

78. Linda E. Saltzman, PhD, Amy Levenson, MD, and Jack C. Smith, MS, "Suicides Among Persons 15–24 Years of Age, 1970–1984," Vol. 37, No. SS–1, p. 61.

79. National Center for Injury Prevention and Control, "Injury Prevention: Meeting the Challenge," p. 253.

80. Kochanek and Hudson, p. 23.

81. Saltzman, et al., p. 61.

82. Kochanek and Hudson, p. 23.

83. Blumenthal and Kupfer, p. 257, and Jeffrey H. Boyd, MD, MPH, and Eve K. Moscicki, ScD, MPH, "Firearms and Youth Suicide," *American Journal of Public Health*, October 1986, Vol. 76, No. 10, p. 1240.

84. Jeffrey H. Boyd, MD, MPH, "The Increasing Rate of Suicide By Firearms," *New England Journal of Medicine*, 1983, Vol. 308, p. 872, Laurie Duker, MPPM, *Firearm Facts: Youth Suicide and Guns*, Arlington, VA: National Center for Education in Maternal and Child Health, and Boyd and Moscicki, "Firearms and Youth Suicide," p. 1240.

85. National Center for Injury Prevention and Control, "Injury Prevention: Meeting the Challenge," p. 253.

86. "Suicide Among Children, Adolescents, and Young Adults—United States, 1980–1992," *Morbidity and Mortality Weekly Report*, April 21, 1995, Vol. 44, No. 15, p. 289.

87. Duker, *Firearm Facts: Youth Suicide and Guns*.

88. "Suicide Among Children, Adolescents, and Young Adults—United States, 1980–1992," p. 289.

89. Moscicki and Boyd, "Epidemiologic Trends in Firearm Suicides among Adolescents," p. 59.

90. Louis Harris, *A Survey of Experience, Perceptions, And Apprehensions About Guns Among Young People in America*, prepared for the Harvard School of Public Health, conducted by LH Research, Inc., July 1993, p. 12.

91. Harris, p. vi.

92. "Guns by the Numbers," p. 3A.

93. Talmey-Drake Research & Strategy, Inc., *The Family Safety Survey: A National Survey of Parents' Compliance with the Family Safety Check*, prepared for the National SAFE KIDS Campaign, May 8, 1995, p. 11.

94. Rosenberg, Mercy and Houk, p. 3030.

95. Blumenthal and Kupfer, p. 264.

96. Blumenthal and Kupfer, p. 264, Garland and Zigler, p. 172, and Rosenberg, Mercy, and Houk, p. 3030.

97. Rosenberg and Fenley, p. 186.

98. Moscicki and Boyd, "Epidemiologic Trends in Firearm Suicides among Adolescents," p. 53, and Glick, p. 43.

99. Moscicki and Boyd, "Epidemiologic Trends in Firearm Suicides among Adolescents," p. 53.

100. Glick, p. 43.

101. Weed, pp. 139, 145.

102. Moscicki and Boyd, "Epidemiologic Trends in Firearm Suicides among Adolescents," p. 53.

103. Saltzman, et al., p. 65.

104. Glick, pp. 1, 5.

105. Glick, p. 41.

106. "Firearm-Related Years of Potential Life Lost Before Age 65 Years—United States, 1980–1991," *Morbidity and Mortality Weekly Report*, August 26, 1994, Vol. 43, No. 33, pp. 609–610.

107. "Firearm-Related Years of Potential Life Lost Before Age 65 Years—United States, 1980–1991," p. 610.

108. Garen J. Wintemute, MD, MPH, *Trauma in Transition: Trends in Deaths from Firearm and Motor Vehicle Injuries*, Davis, CA: Violence Prevention Research Program, University of California, Davis, January 1995, Press Release.

109. Garen J. Wintemute, MD, MPH, and Mona A. Wright, BS, "Initial and Subsequent Hospital Costs of Firearm Injuries," *Journal of Trauma*, October 1992, Vol. 33, No. 4, p. 556.

110. Wintemute and Wright, p. 556.

111. Wintemute and Wright, p. 557.

112. Wintemute and Wright, "Initial and Subsequent Hospital Costs of Firearm Injuries," p. 557.

5

Heavy Metal Music Contributes to Teen Suicide

Raymond Kuntz, Sam Brownback, and Joseph Lieberman

Raymond Kuntz's teenage son committed suicide in 1996 while listening to a CD by the heavy metal group Marilyn Manson. Kuntz testified November 6, 1997, on the effects of heavy metal music on teen suicide before the U.S. Senate's Committee on Governmental Affairs Subcommittee on Oversight of Governmental Management, Restructuring, and the District of Columbia. Senator Sam Brownback of Kansas is the subcommittee's chair and Senator Joseph Lieberman of Connecticut is a ranking member of the subcommittee. Both senators are actively involved in investigating the effect of violent lyrics on youth and in encouraging music corporations to take responsibility for those lyrics.

Heavy metal music glorifies death and encourages violence and suicide among teenagers. The offensive lyrics found in heavy metal music contradict community values, harm society, and endanger the nation's children. Music corporation executives should take responsibility for the harm that comes to their impressionable listeners. Furthermore, parental advisory labels should be mandatory on the covers of all violent and offensive music.

For the record, my name is Raymond Kuntz, and our family calls Burlington, North Dakota, home. I have traveled to Washington, D.C., from there today to speak to you all regarding an issue that has changed our lives forever: Violent music's impact on our children.

On the morning of December 12, 1996, as part of our family's normal daily behavior, my wife started our son's shower for him and then went to wake him. But Richard, our son, was not sleeping in his bed. He was dead. He had killed himself. Richard has left us, and he is never coming back.

Please listen to what Richard heard as he died, hear what was in his mind, the lyrics to Marilyn Manson's "The Reflecting God" from the CD titled *Antichrist Superstar*.

> Your world is an ashtray
> We burn and coil like cigarettes

Reprinted from testimony given by Raymond Kuntz before the U.S. Senate Committee on Governmental Affairs, Subcommittee on Oversight of Government Management, Restructuring, and the District of Columbia, Washington, D.C., November 6, 1997.

The more you cry your ashes turn to mud
Its the nature of the leeches, the Virgin's feeling cheated
You've only spent a second of you're life
My world is unaffected, there is an exit here
I say it is and then it's true, there is a dream inside a dream
I'm wide awake the more I sleep
You'll understand when I'm dead
l went to God just to see, and I was looking at me
Saw heaven and hell were lies
When I'm God everyone dies
Scar, can you feel my power?
Shoot here and the world gets smaller
Scar
Scar
Can you feel my power
One shot and the world gets smaller
Let's jump upon the sharp swords
And cut away our smiles
Without the threat of death
There's no reason to live at all
My world is unaffected, there is an exit here
I say it is and then it's true
There is a dream inside a dream
I'm wide awake the more I sleep
You'll understand when I'm dead.

Dear sirs, my son was listening to Marilyn Manson's *Antichrist Superstar* on his stereo when he died—I personally removed that CD with the red lightning bolt on it from his player the next day—with the rough draft of an English class paper about this artist that had been returned to him that very day for final revisions, on the stand next to his body. Richard's friends tell us that in the end this song, "The Reflecting God," from that CD was his favorite song. They say that this song was what he always seemed to be listening to whenever they came over, and the lyrics of that song read as an unequivocally direct inducement to take one's own life.

The lyrics of this song contributed directly to my son's death.

If you do not believe me, listen to the bridge in the chorus of "The Reflecting God" as performed, not as written in the liner notes: "Each thing I show you is a piece of my death"; "One shot and the world gets smaller"; "Shoot here and the world gets smaller"; "Shoot shoot shoot motherfucker/Shoot shoot shoot motherfucker"; "No salvation, no forgiveness/This is beyond your experience"; "No salvation, no forgiveness, no salvation."

Gentlemen, we are all certainly free to make our own decisions regarding the value of content. But if you were to ask me, I would say that the lyrics to this song contributed directly to my son's death.

Additionally, two of my son's friends, who have been treated for attempted suicide since his death, are and were caught up in Marilyn Manson's fearful, frightening music and are still considered to be at risk.

Sirs, this music, because it glorifies intolerance and hate, and promotes suicide, contradicts all of the community values that people of good will, regardless of faith, ideology, race, economic or social position, share. Simply put, this music hurts us as a people. Our children are quietly being destroyed (dying), by this man's music, by ones and twos in scattered isolation throughout our nation today.

This artist's own words, in his lyrics and interviews, and his actions, indicate that this injury to society is intentional. The predatory world that Brian Warner markets, through his stage persona as Marilyn Manson, is a world no normal person would wish to live in.

Brian Warner's band members have adopted androgynous, two-part stage names, the first part derived from a female celebrity and the second part from a convicted male mass murderer. And Brian got lucky; as the lead, he got to pick "Marilyn" from Marilyn Monroe, the female celebrity who committed suicide, and "Manson" from Charles Manson, mass murderer.

Corporations should be responsible

By their natures, corporations do not have consciences, and it is understandable that MCA would wish to defend a product that entered the Billboard 200 chart at No. 3. But even though they are soulless, corporations do have social obligations and responsibilities.

I understand that the lyrics to individual songs and the content of interviews made by artists with obscure magazines and newsletters are below a CEO's event horizon. But somewhere down the hierarchy line, someone who is aware of both artistic content and stated intent is making corporate economic decisions driven by greed that kill. Corporate decision-making that kills.

Shaming major corporations into more responsible behavior is good. But forcing a corporation to divest itself of a socially unacceptable, still functional subset, possibly at a profit, does nothing to rectify the problem or wash clean the hands of those involved.

From my experience, and based on the fact that you have seen the need to convene this hearing, there is no question in my mind that the damage that this music is doing to our children is a serious problem in our country today.

I believe we need to make the voluntary RIAA [Recording Industry Association of America] parental advisory sticker program mandatory so that parents, moms and dads, can better monitor their children's listening to help keep dangerous materials out of their hands.

From what my family has experienced, this music is a cancer on our society. I have given you my ideas of what we can do to solve this problem and stress that we must act as a people to protect our children from the twin evils of murder and suicide.

Sirs, if there is anything you can do about this problem, my wife, Christine, and I are ready to help you in any way that we can.

Thank you.

Senator Sam Brownback. Thank you, Mr. Kuntz, for your very touching testimony, and thank you for your courage at being here.

I understand that your son, as you stated in your testimony, was doing a paper for his English class on Marilyn Manson?

Mr. Kuntz. Yes, he was.

Senator Brownback. Could you or would you care to share any of the thoughts that your son was writing at that time in that English paper?

Mr. Kuntz. If my son were still alive today, I would say that I believe from the contents of this paper that he was starting to mature, even though it is in a school boy's language, that he was starting to mature intellectually and was beginning to grasp and understand social values that we all share, because the paper addresses these kinds of things. But my son is dead, and I really do not know what to think of this paper.

The English paper

A line from the paper: "His album projects an image of hate towards the Christian community, and the drugs he uses publicly are mind-degrading."

"Throughout his set, he rips and tears at his jagged clothes until naked except for a leather jockstrap. Then he grabs a bottle, breaks it over his head, and invites the crowd to shower him in spit." In a world of AIDS, is that a wise idea?

"Manson's second album *Smells Like Children* is a tribute to two tracks, 'abuse' (part one and two) and 'confusion' which were on the original cut but were . . . taken off the album before it was distributed. Manson explains the reason for this in an interview with Rudolf; 'both tracks' featured collaborations done sometime last year with a guy named Tony Wiggins. It involved illegal activities."

My son's closing: "Through the tolerance of 'evil' groups such as Marilyn Manson, many children's minds are being degraded. Marilyn Manson shows that it is possible for a Christian society to produce somebody who is against everything it stands for. Believing that what he is doing is good and promoting it through music, he gains followers by epitomizing children's black thoughts of rebellion."

Senator Brownback. Did you talk with your son's friends about coming here to testify?

Mr. Kuntz. Yes, I did.

Senator Brownback. What did they think about you testifying on your son's suicide?

Mr. Kuntz. Our son's friends have been a great source of comfort for us. They come to our home and visit us. They stop by the store and talk to me. We comfort them; they comfort us. And I have talked to them extensively about this kind of music and what I plan to do. I have asked them if this is proper, if they approve of what I am doing, and part of the reason that I am here today is because they tell me that what I am doing is the right thing to do.

Senator Brownback. How did they respond to this whole ordeal? You mentioned that they came by your store and spoke with you. Right after this happened, how did they respond to the whole ordeal?

Mr. Kuntz. They were horrified and surprised and couldn't understand and terribly hurt. I found out something about our society then. We really do care for each other. We care for our family; we care for our friends and neighbors. Our children do, too. Nobody wants to experience this kind of loss.

Senator Brownback. Did you know your son was listening to this type of music, Mr. Kuntz?

Mr. Kuntz. Yes, as a matter of fact, I did. I talked to my son as long as—well, it would be three years ago now—about the heavy metal music that he listened to. I didn't care for the liner art. I didn't care for the titles of the songs. I didn't care for the lyrics as I read them. And one day I had a talk with him. He was an aggressive roller-blader, a really athletic boy, and he had a ramp built and some other stuff. And he had symbols on there that I didn't care for, things like swastikas and anarchist symbols and this sort of stuff. And I talked to him about the music and where the symbols were coming from and told him that I didn't want him to use those symbols because I didn't want him to become desensitized by casual exposure to symbols that have a very real, historical association with evil. And he painted them out, and things went on.

And two years ago, when he was 13, we came back from the lake and a camping trip, and he talked to me afterwards, and he said, "Dad," he said, "you know, you don't like some of the music that I listen to, but some of the kids down there were listening to stuff that I found offensive." And I said, "What was that, honey?" And he said, "White Zombie and Marilyn Manson." And I said, "Well, what did you do?" He says, "Well, I took them away and I wouldn't let them listen to them."

Well, sir, I am afraid that he took those albums away from those children and brought them into his own life. I thought my son, when he told me this story, was making headway towards maturity.

This music, because it glorifies intolerance and hate, and promotes suicide, contradicts all of the community values that people of good will, regardless of faith, ideology, race, economic or social position, share.

Senator Brownback. Have you talked with other parents in North Dakota or your community or around the country that have experienced something similar to what your family has experienced?

Mr. Kuntz. No, not directly. We have had other suicides in the community. Every child who suicides is a different person with a different life, not necessarily associated with this kind of music. There was a suicide four months after my son's death where a young man drove his car off a cliff on the way back from a neighboring community, coming back from some heavy metal concert. I don't know who it was. But as far as talking to parents about it, no, I haven't.

People who have experienced suicide in their lives that are survivors rarely talk to other people. They will occasionally. They will open themselves and talk to somebody who has experienced suicide, but not to the general community. And it is amazing how much there is out there.

Senator Brownback. I hope your testimony will embolden and empower some of those parents to be willing to talk about what has to be a terribly anguishing, just gut-wrenching experience. And I would invite them to

contact this Subcommittee if there are others that want to speak out about
it. I appreciate your candor and your courage in coming forward.

Senator Lieberman.

Senator Joseph Lieberman. Thanks, Mr. Chairman.

Mr. Kuntz, I very much appreciate your coming here. I was so struck
by your letter when you sent it to me earlier in the year about what you
had been through, and it has got to be—it is, obviously, very, very painful
to recount this tragedy that you and your family have undergone. And I
admire you for having the courage to do it. Each of us who are parents
can feel what you are feeling, and it is terrifying. It is a nightmare.

---

*The damage that this music is doing to our children
is a serious problem in our country today.*

I know your hope is—and I admire you tremendously for this—that it
is worth coming forward and telling your story as a warning to other
people and to try to help us do something about it, and in a way today to
give you the opportunity to speak directly to some of the people in the
recording industry, who are good people but are part of producing some
terrible music that you have reason to believe helped to end your son's life.

I was thinking, as you were reading from his paper, which was quite
eloquent—and I apologize if this seems like a digression; I am going to do
it very briefly—but it so movingly speaks to a concern that I think moti-
vates so much of our effort here and the reflections your son had about
the contrast between what Marilyn Manson music was doing and religion, in this case Christianity.

I talked about a values vacuum in my testimony. There is a wonder-
ful man named Father Richard Neuhaus who has written a book called
The Naked Public Square, in which he describes the extent to which we in
our country, sometimes for good reasons, have nonetheless pushed out of
the public square acceptance and respect of one of the major sources of
values and discipline in our culture traditionally, which is religion, beyond constitutional reasons, and that what happens then when the public square is naked is that something else fills it. And too often in our time
what is filling it is this abominable culture, music, TV, movies, too much
of it giving our kids exactly the wrong message.

Look, we are an imperfect species, human beings. We strive to maintain our stability and to improve ourselves. And the influences on us,
whether they set standards and help us conduct our lives, or whether
they destroy our ability to do so, have a major impact on how we as individuals and how our overall society goes forward.

And your testimony is just the most stunning evidence of that that I
have heard in a long time, quite explicitly—I mean, down to the title of
the CD that your son was listening to.

The parents' responsibility

I want to just ask you one or two questions. As you know, a lot of people
in the record industry who have spoken out on this problem say, yes,

some of this music is awful, but the artists, so-called, have a First Amendment right to have their music produced. And the real responsibility here is on parents to monitor what music their kids are listening to.

How do you respond to that argument?

Mr. Kuntz. We all have a responsibility to look after our children, not just parents but the political establishment, the churches, the schools, the corporate world, the business community. If we don't look after our children, our society is ultimately not going to make it. It is a joint thing. Nobody is exempt from responsibility here. We all share it.

Senator Lieberman. So parents really can't do it alone.

Mr. Kuntz. It is impossible to do it alone.

Senator Lieberman. Right. I agree. I am from Connecticut so—I have been to North Dakota. Senator Conrad talks to me about it all the time. But some of the perverse behavior that is celebrated in music such as we are focused on today, it has always existed. But traditionally, in the history of the human race, it has been in the shadows. It has been concealed. And part of what has happened in our time is that vile material like this gets produced, gets mass marketed, it is on television; it is in the movies, and your son in Burlington, North Dakota, not in some dark alley in one of America's big cities, gets to tap into the lowest, most degrading aspects of our culture. And it really is part of why—I think you are absolutely right. Parents can't do it themselves, no matter where they live. Nobody is safe. There are no sanctuaries anymore. And that is why we have to go back to the top of the corporations that are producing this and ask the executives to be responsible.

I failed to recognize that my son was holding a hand grenade and it was live and that it was going to go off in his mind.

Let me ask one final question that goes to the comment you made about the existing record industry association labeling system. You touched on some of this briefly in response to Senator Brownback. I think you said to Senator Brownback that you knew that your son had Marilyn Manson CDs or albums. Did you know what was on those albums?

Mr. Kuntz. No. I was aware that my son was writing this English class paper on Marilyn Manson. I wasn't aware until then that he was listening to it. We skipped from the incident at the camping to writing this paper about Marilyn Manson, and I thought that he was doing an intellectual, academic exercise. And my little boy, about two weeks before he died, he brought this—he said, "Daddy, come here." He had me come into his bedroom, and he said, "Here, this is the 'Antichrist Superstar' CD that I am doing for my English class paper." And I looked at it, and I looked at the flip side, looked at the liner art, and I looked at the text, and I blew up, told him I didn't want this stuff in my house. And after talking with my wife and my son—and my wife had talked with the English teacher, who I believe was blindsided by the—I don't believe she had any idea whatsoever what the contents of this stuff was. I let it slide.

But I missed an opportunity there. I failed my son as a father. My son came to me and said, "Daddy, Daddy, look what I have." And I failed to recognize that my son was holding a hand grenade and it was live and that it was going to go off in his mind.

I wish to this day that I had been a reasonable and rational person and sat down and gone over the lyrics with him and talked about it and reached out and touched my son, and perhaps what he was doing would have remained an academic exercise.

Senator Lieberman. I understand how you feel, but don't be too hard on yourself. Almost every parent in America in that position would have done exactly what you did because it didn't look like a hand grenade. It looked like a CD. Unfortunately, it was a hand grenade.

I thank you from the bottom of my heart for having the guts to come forward and tell this story. I wish you and your wife and family well. Thank you.

6

Depression Contributes to Suicide

Andrew E. Slaby and Lili Frank Garfinkel

Andrew E. Slaby is a psychiatrist in New York specializing in depression and crisis intervention. Lili Frank Garfinkel is a freelance writer. They are the authors of No One Saw My Pain: Why Teens Kill Themselves.

Approximately 10 percent of high school students suffer from depression and an unknown number are never even diagnosed. For many of these teens, the mental pain of depression is so overwhelming that they believe the only way they can end their anguish is to commit suicide. Although depression is recognized, understood, and treated more than ever before, family, friends, and health care professionals frequently overlook or downplay clues that a depressed teen is considering suicide. With proper intervention and treatment, however, many depressed teens can overcome their suicidal tendencies.

The current statistics on youth suicide continue to be frightening. More than 5,000 youth under the age of twenty-five kill themselves in the United States every year. Of these, 2,000 are teenagers.[1] And for every completed suicide between 300 and 350 serious attempts are made.[2] Surveys have shown that as many as 60 percent of all high school students have thought about their own death or about killing themselves.[3] In addition, one out of every ten high school students experiences some form of severe depression during the high school years.[4]

I have counseled depressed teens and their families for the last twenty years. In that time I have made every effort to reach out to teachers, clergy, and counselors, as well as many other professionals concerned with the well-being of young people. My patients have included teens in crisis, young people preoccupied with morbid thoughts, teens who have made suicidal gestures or those who have actually attempted suicide, and most tragically, family members who have lost a teen to suicide. I feel tremendous relief and hope when I am able to intervene successfully with young people in crisis and their families. Whether I am directly involved in the therapeutic process or facilitate connection with other community resources, sparing as many people as possible the most severe consequences of depression remains my ongoing goal.

The mental pain of depression

Depression is commonly portrayed unidimensionally as profound, all-encompassing sadness. When I ask adults and teens how they would conceptualize a depressed person, they most often describe a hollow-eyed, miserable person who sleepwalks through life before taking an overdose. There is no understanding or recognition of the rage, the fear, and the insurmountable pain that are so much a part of depression. Imagine the worst physical pain you've ever had—a broken bone, a toothache, or labor pain—multiply it tenfold and take away the cause; then you can possibly approximate the pain of depression. The mental pain of depression is so all-consuming that it becomes impossible to derive any pleasure or satisfaction from life; no interests can stimulate attention and perseverance, no persons can adequately foster love or loyalty. The world is seen as bleak and gray. To someone who is profoundly depressed, the option of suicide becomes the only option, the only way to control life and end the unremitting pain.

To someone who is profoundly depressed, the option of suicide becomes the only option, the only way to control life and end the unremitting pain.

Depression is a term that has been too loosely integrated into our vocabulary. When we say "I'm so depressed about . . ." and yet continue to function, work, play, interact with people, it means we're temporarily unhappy about something. Clinical depression, however, is not so transient. A diagnosis of depression is measurable according to specific characteristics, which include sleep disturbance (insomnia or sleeping all the time), changes in eating habits (overeating or lack of appetite), inability to concentrate, physical symptoms (such as headaches, stomachaches), agitation or fatigue, and wretched, morbid thoughts about oneself and the future.[5]

The pain of depression can be far more overwhelming, more incapacitating, than any physical pain. Individuals who are hurting emotionally think poorly of themselves and act in ways that will cause others to think poorly of them. As this cycle is perpetuated, they become more and more isolated and convinced of their worthlessness. It is understandable, then, that persons who are depressed engage in antisocial or delinquent behavior, develop unusually hostile relationships with those closest to them, or experience progressive difficulties with peer relationships. What they are really doing is creating in the minds of others the same negative impressions they already feel about themselves.

Options like reaching out and seeking help are rarely considered or are rejected outright, and as the depression evolves the only option that promises to shut off the pain is suicide.

The impact of depression

Clinical depression impacts people in real physiological as well as emotional ways. For a diagnosis of clinical depression to be made, it must last at least two weeks and include at least five of the following symptoms: the inability to concentrate, feelings of hopelessness, changes in regular eating habits, sleep disturbances, loss or lack of energy, behavioral changes (restlessness and agitation), engaging in risk-taking behaviors, changes in schoolwork and/or work habits, and thoughts of suicide. Often there is a decrease in sexual energy. In fact, depressed teens may turn to others through sexual encounters in order to gain some acceptance and positive feedback.

It is typical for people with depression to perceive life in an almost totally distorted and negative way, so that thinking and behavior become radically altered. Both one's past history and day-to-day life are rewritten and recast so that everything is seen in the bleakest terms.

It is estimated that approximately one in ten high school students can be diagnosed with depression at some time in his or her life.

It is estimated that approximately one in ten high school students can be diagnosed with depression at some time in his or her life. Many more are never identified. For some fortunate persons, an episode of clinical depression, even untreated, will pass without any lingering effects. For others, therapy and a course of antidepressant medication will be necessary. In either case, most teens who have depression do not go on to attempt or commit suicide. The pressing questions are: Can we determine which kids are more likely to attempt or commit suicide? What separates those people who live with depression from those who are preoccupied with thoughts about suicide, those who make specific plans to kill themselves, or those who actually carry out their plans or impulsively commit suicide?

Through "psychological autopsies" of teens who killed themselves or attempted to do so this viewpoint identifies those "markers" or features that predispose young people not only to depression but also to suicide. Some of these markers are: a family history of depression or suicide; learning disabilities (primarily because impulsivity is a quality common to both suicide and certain learning disabilities); a history of physical, sexual, or emotional abuse; delinquency; substance abuse; and recurrent, long-lasting episodes of depression.

At some time in our lives we all experience morbid thoughts, thoughts about our own death and the impact our death would have on those around us. Children begin to have these thoughts at an early age, usually around age four, and then again at different times as they mature. Usually these thoughts are transient and not likely to be associated with suicidal behavior. In rare cases, children might be preoccupied with thoughts of death and dying when a grandparent dies, even if a pet dies. They want to join the departed one in heaven. I have interviewed some very young children who have made primitive suicidal gestures for this reason.

Children and teenagers who experience depression at a young age may become dependent on others for affirmation of their very being. Instead of recognizing their own self-worth, they rely on others to provide them with positive feelings. They become needy, dependent, vulnerable teens and adults. Their pathway to help and healing is paved with missed cues and frustration.

Young persons who actually formulate a plan for their own suicide may not tell a soul of their plans, or they may swear a single trusted friend to secrecy about their intentions. Some teens even boast in a cavalier or indirect way about how they will one day kill themselves. They may give away treasured possessions; they may write unusually emotional letters to friends or an essay on suicide for English class. These behaviors should be viewed with alarm and clearly warrant immediate counseling and treatment.

Suicidal gestures and attempts

When we talk about suicidal gestures, we are referring to attention-seeking behaviors, real cries for help. A suicidal gesture is a deliberate act of self-injury without the intention of dying. Gestures may include ingesting a nonlethal number of pills, self-injury such as minor wrist-slashing, or even waving a firearm around in front of friends. Teens who wave red flags in these ways may not want to die; yet, deaths have been known to occur in spite of the lack of intention.

Suicide attempts are really failed suicides. Some young persons are fortunate enough to be accidentally saved from killing themselves: They are found hanging, but alive, or survive a gunshot wound, or are revived from an overdose. The intent to kill themselves may persist, and they may try again, even succeed. On the other hand, some rescued teens view their survival as a sign that they were not meant to die, and with help they truly begin to work on dealing with their depression.

Any significant crisis related to depression, regardless of how it may manifest itself, should be viewed as a statement about the stresses in a young person's life, a lack of coping mechanisms, and/or society's response to his or her behaviors and problems at that time. The ultimate crisis precipitating the suicide attempt may reflect a breakdown at all three levels: stress and conflict, coping, and societal response.

Adolescent depression is recognized, diagnosed, and treated more frequently than even five years ago. And yet the escalating statistics of adolescent suicide seem to nullify any serious progress.

Today, depression is better understood than ever before. It is a biological vulnerability that surfaces when sufficiently disturbing life experiences occur. It lies dormant in some individuals only to occur or recur when negative events come to bear on the vulnerable person. Depression alters the individual's functioning, creating additional problems. For instance, lacking the energy or desire to do constructive activities, the depressed teen frequently shows a deterioration in school and social functioning.

Adolescent depression is recognized, diagnosed, and treated more frequently than even five years ago. And yet the escalating statistics of adolescent suicide seem to nullify any serious progress. It is ironic that in an age where the cult of youth is so valued, emulated, and pursued, we have been unable to respond to our children and teens when they are in the greatest pain.

Suicide is most often the fatal end point of depression.

This generation of teens will have to learn and integrate—if they haven't already—a whole new system of strategies to cope with the complexity and variety of our societal and cultural norms. Whereas historically the family, the church, and the community frequently provided a safety net for children, where they were nurtured and sheltered and where certain types of behaviors were sanctioned and reinforced, this is no longer the case. Family breakdown, family and community violence, economic instability, stress, drugs—all are far too familiar to teens growing up today. And yet, these are still children, and developmentally they are not ready to face these formidable pressures. Ultimately, the crises that do confront many children who are depressed represent the convergence of complex stressors, immature and ineffectual coping mechanisms, and a lack of societal response.

Did no one see the pain?

It is hard to express the pain and poignancy I feel when meeting with families of children who have killed themselves. Whether we meet a week after the suicide or ten years later, I feel connected and bound by the need to help them understand what happened and go on with their lives. I am very aware that, no matter what insight I may help them discover, no matter what resolution or peace they may find in their lives, it will not be enough—they will struggle with guilt and with self-recriminations forever.

In nearly every case of suicide I have reviewed, clues to the adolescent's plans were overlooked or downplayed. They weren't intentionally missed, but unknowingly missed. This does not necessarily mean that the suicide could have been prevented. *Some people will kill themselves no matter what intervention takes place.* In my mind, many adolescent patients remain vulnerable; I worry and wonder how they will respond five or ten years from now, when a crisis may arise and other pressures and circumstances may influence their responses. The histories of many adults who have committed suicide include episodes of severe depression, if not suicide attempts, during adolescence.

Why were the clues missed? Family members and friends did not understand the enormity of the changes they were seeing. They focused on the consequences and not on the underlying problem, so that "family problems" or "drug use" or "anorexia" became the diagnosis. Sometimes the anger, the confusion, and the irritability were treated, but not the depression. The underlying problem remained, torturous and festering.

Were their cries not heard? No, something was heard: Chad's silence, Sarah's continuous crying, Carly's rage, Tim's reactions to an abusive father, Kent's mental illness, David's drug use, and John's anxiety about his sexuality. Only in hindsight, however, do we realize that somehow the responses to their crises were not effective.

In the midst of a crisis, it is usually difficult to judge whether the choices that are made are the right ones, if the therapy is working, or if the medicine or counseling has helped. It is hard to stand back and say: Is this helping? If not, why? When the behaviors have not changed after a reasonable amount of time, some thought should be given to, at the very least, asking the treatment personnel some probing questions or seeking another opinion. Too often, parents are loath to ask these questions of professionals; they are intimidated and fear being blamed. Nevertheless, they must be assertive.

Among professionals there needs to be a greater understanding of the medical aspect of psychiatric illness that coexists with the psychological forces. Pediatricians, family doctors, internists, and emergency-room physicians must have more intensive training in treating depression. The same energy that we have brought to training students about AIDS and safe sex should be brought to providing knowledge about depression in all its guises. Drug abuse, risk-taking behaviors, promiscuity, and social isolation should provoke questions about suicidal thought and intentions. If we can save more young people it will be worth it.

Depression is a very treatable illness; the social, academic, and personal problems resulting from depression are much harder to alleviate.

Suicide is most often the fatal end point of depression, substance abuse, and delinquency. When one sees a pattern that often ends in suicide, immediate attention must be directed to the teen's safety. Hospitalization of the acutely suicidal adolescent is not optional; it cannot be postponed until tomorrow. The young person must be safe, and if the family cannot trust the child over the course of the day and night, then twenty-four-hour care in a hospital is mandatory. If an outpatient level of care is thought to be acceptable, the home must be made suicide-proof. This can never be completely accomplished; however, I ask parents to remove all firearms, dispose of all unused medicines, lock up the keys to the cars, and remove all ropes or cords that could be used for hanging. Making the method for self-destruction less accessible gives the teen more time to consider options other than suicide.

Treatment outside of the hospital most often involves three components: crisis intervention, counseling, and medication. Crisis intervention includes specific actions that adults can take to alleviate the immediate conflicts and problems facing the teenager. If it's a failing grade, work with the school to give an incomplete in the class. If it's parent-child conflict about a specific issue, address the disagreements in counseling. Problems need to be defused.

At one time counseling was synonymous with psychoanalytic therapy, which required a careful examination of the individual's past in order to gain insight into present behavior. Now we know that two types of counseling work best for depression—interpersonal and cognitive behavioral therapies. Interpersonal therapy examines and develops new ways of interacting with others so that fewer negative consequences occur when the depressed person interfaces with others. Cognitive behavioral therapy enables the client to acquire new verbal and mental strategies in self-directing current and future behaviors. Depressed teens don't have to fear facing their past alone to assure improvement. Today counseling is less disturbing and more practical than psychoanalysis.

Counseling addresses the behavioral and interactional problems resulting from the underlying depression. The most effective treatment, however, is a combination of medication and counseling. The original antidepressants had an array of side effects that made them very unpleasant to take. No longer do patients need to fear side effects such as constipation, blurred vision, lowered blood pressure, and dry mouth. The most recently developed antidepressants appear to be both safe and relatively free of side effects.

Patience is essential when the teen is taking an antidepressant. It may take one or two trials of different medicines to find the right one. It may take as long as four to six weeks for the teen to respond to the antidepressant. Moreover, the dose must be optimum. Probably two of the most common medication mistakes are giving too low a dose and giving it for an inadequate length of time.

Depression is a very treatable illness; the social, academic, and personal problems resulting from depression are much harder to alleviate.

Notes

1. Centers for Disease Control (1985). *Suicide surveillance* 1970–1980. Atlanta: U.S. Department of Health and Human Services, Public Health Service, Violent Epidemiology Branch, Center for Health Promotion and Education.

2. Garfinkel, B.D. (1986). Major affective disorders in children and adolescents. In G. Winokur & P. Clayton (Eds.), *The medical basis of psychiatry*. Philadelphia: Saunders.

3. Kandel, D., Raveis, V., & Davies, M. (1991). Suicidal ideation in adolescence: Depression, substance use, and other risk factors. *Journal of Youth and Adolescence* 20:289–309.

4. McCracken, J.T. (1992). The epidemiology of child and adolescent mood disorders. *Child and Adolescent Psychiatric Clinics of North America* 1(1):53–73. Philadelphia: Saunders.

5. American Psychiatric Association (1994). *Diagnostic and statistical manual of mental disorders* (DSM-IV). Washington, D.C.: Author.

7

Substance Abuse Is a Factor in Many Suicides

David Lester

David Lester is a professor of psychology at Richard Stockton College of New Jersey. He has written numerous articles and books about teen suicide, including The Cruelest Death: The Enigma of Adolescent Suicide *and* Making Sense of Suicide: An In-Depth Look at Why People Kill Themselves.

The consumption of alcohol and/or drugs is frequently a contributing factor to suicide. Alcohol and drugs increase feelings of depression and isolation, ease fears of death, and reduce inhibitions about suicide. Furthermore, alcohol and drugs are frequently used as a means of committing suicide.

No cause-and-effect relationship has been established between suicide and the use of alcohol and/or drugs, but the consumption of these agents is often a contributing factor to suicide for several reasons. The use of alcohol and drugs may lower inhibitions and impair judgment of a person contemplating suicide and therefore make the act more likely, and alcohol and drug use aggravate other risk factors for suicide such as depression. Furthermore, because drugs are potentially lethal and relatively easy to obtain and use, they are often used as instruments of self-destruction. However, because it has been only relatively recently that large numbers of people have begun to use drugs to deliberately induce mood changes (as alcohol has been used for centuries), we do not have much information about how they relate to suicide. Perhaps this is due, in part, to the fact that people are typically more secretive about their drug use than they are about alcohol use. Moreover, different drugs have very different effects, and it may not be possible to draw conclusions that apply to all drugs.

One way in which drugs are thought to be different from alcohol, at least in the popular press, is that particular drugs are sometimes thought to *cause* suicide. For example, when Art Linkletter's daughter killed herself by jumping out of a window (allegedly, she thought she had the ability to fly), her father blamed her death on the LSD that she was high on and that she regularly used. After her death, Linkletter worked hard warning young people to stay away from the drugs that he felt killed his daughter. Linkletter's simplistic analysis, that attributed his daughter's suicide only to drug use, ignored her long history of disturbed behavior, including her very early and unhappy marriage.

In this viewpoint, I will examine the research findings about the effects of drugs and alcohol on suicidal behavior. As has been my practice in this book, I will not draw conclusions from single, incompletely reported cases like the one mentioned above, but instead will look at evidence gathered from large groups of suicidal people.

Alcoholism, drug abuse, and suicide

Alcoholism—genuine physical and psychological addiction to alcohol—was considered by Karl Menninger (1938) to be a form of suicidal behavior. The alcoholic way of life is clearly a self-destructive course. Real physiological damage can occur to the drinker's liver and brain. Jobs and social relationships are often destroyed, leaving the alcoholic with only the companionship of other heavy drinkers. Menninger called this type of behavior *chronic suicide* and saw it as motivated by the same self-destructive (though possibly unconscious) urges as suicide. Alternatively, suicide and alcoholism (and perhaps drug abuse as well) may be expressions of the same underlying causal variable, such as a history of social disorganization.

Substance abusers appear to have a higher incidence of both completed and attempted suicide than nonabusers (Lester, 1992). This may be because substance abuse has the following effects: it can disrupt social relationships and impair work performance, which leads to social isolation and social decline; it can increase impulsivity and lower restraints against self-harmful acts; it can increase self-deprecation and depressive tendencies that may increase the probability of suicidal behavior (Roy and Linnoila, 1986). Also, if a person is either a chronic alcoholic or acutely intoxicated, when he takes drugs, their effect can be much more lethal to the body.

Drugs as an instrument of suicide

Drugs are frequently used for committing suicide. From 1960 to 1980, the average suicide rate of 16 major nations of the world rose from 11.8 per 100,000 deaths per year to 14.8. The average rate of suicide for deaths that resulted from the ingestion of solid and liquid substances rose during this period from 2.3 to 3.0 (Lester, 1990). In the United States in 1980, the use of solid and liquid substances was the third most common method for suicide, after firearms and hanging (Baker et al., 1984) and in 1989, an analysis of 100,000 deaths found positive blood alcohol concentration (BAC) in 35 percent of suicide fatalities (National Committee for Injury Prevention and Control, 1993).

In developed nations, the majority of those using solid and liquid substances to commit suicide take them in the form of medications. (In developing nations, chemical fertilizers and insecticides are more commonly used.) Antidepressants are now the medications most frequently used for committing suicide, especially because physicians have become more cautious in prescribing barbiturates, once used in many suicidal deaths (Retterstol, 1993). However, the more recently developed antidepressants, such as Mianserin (a British drug), are much less likely to cause accidental and suicidal deaths than the older antidepressants, such as Elavil (amitriptyline) (Leonard, 1988).

The consumption of [alcohol and/or drugs] is often a contributing factor to suicide.

There is good evidence that by making particular medications less available, it decreases the frequency of their use for suicide (Lester, 1993). For example, the use of barbiturates for suicide in the United States was directly associated with their sales volume (i.e., the more barbiturates were sold, the more they were used for suicide). Similarly, in 1961, in Japan, after laws were passed that made it necessary to have prescriptions to buy barbiturates and other sedatives, their use for suicide dropped.

Reflecting on these findings, Clarke and Lester (1989) have recommended the establishment of the following precautionary measures regarding potentially lethal medications: that doctors limit the number of pills in each prescription; that they prescribe the least toxic medications possible; that they not give automatic refills; that they never write prescriptions unless they have seen and evaluated the patient; that they prescribe suppositories rather than orally taken tablets; and that manufacturers enclose pills in plastic blisters as opposed to loose in a bottle so they are harder to get at, thereby limiting the ability to take large numbers at once. They have also called for the establishment of some sort of central state monitoring system that would detect instances in which people try to fill multiple prescriptions written by different physicians. It should also be able to detect forging and changing of prescriptions by patients.

Drugs that induce suicide

From time to time, claims are made that a particular drug increases the risk of suicide. This claim has been made in the past about medications such as Valium (diazepam), LSD and Prozac (fluoxetine). Every now and then doctors who treat patients with these kinds of medications have a patient who commits suicide. They write a report that gets published in a scientific journal, and when other physicians read it, it encourages them to publish reports of their own similar experiences with medication and suicide. It is important to know, however, that in all cases where suicide has occurred as the result of prescribed medication, research that was based on thousands of individual patient studies did not show evidence that suicide is more common among patients who took the medication. In fact, a recent study found that Prozac is less often accompanied by suicidal behaviors than other antidepressants (Beasley et al., 1992).

Drug automatism

It is sometimes suggested that suicide by drug overdose can occur unintentionally. For example, after taking sleeping pills and falling into a partly conscious state, a person may forget that he has already taken pills and take more to achieve sleep or he may simply take more pills automatically, without being aware of the potentially lethal nature of what he is doing. This hypothetical state of action while being partially conscious has been called "automatism." Drug automatism has been suggested as a cause of occasional deaths through overdose, as in the case of the American writer Jack London, who died of a morphine overdose, a death that some commentators view as accidental and others view as suicidal.

Litman's group (1963) investigated incidents of apparent suicide caused by drugs and they found no evidence that drug automatism played a part in any of the deaths. In another investigation of 94 people who came close to death from drug overdose (Aitken and Proudfoot, 1963), 19 of the patients claimed that the overdose had been taken during an incident of drug automatism. However, after interviewing these people, the researchers concluded that in only two of the cases could the overdose conceivably have been due to automatism. Some of the patients completely denied having ingested drugs; these people tended to be older, to have more often used barbiturates, and to have gone into deeper comas than those who admitted taking drugs.

By making particular medications less available, it decreases the frequency of their use for suicide.

Perhaps the assumption that drug automatism *can* occur stems from the belief that suicide is a deliberate, voluntary act, that will always be remembered and admitted. However, we must not overlook the possibility that patients may lie about their suicide attempts. They may fear that if they admit their attempts, they will be ridiculed, scorned or punished. Even if they do not lie, it is possible that attempters will not remember their acts. Amnesia for the suicidal act can ensue from two causes. First, a physical trauma can easily result in retrograde amnesia—total loss of memory for a period preceding the injury. Somatogenic amnesia characteristically follows accidents in which a person receives a severe blow to the head but it can also result from ingestion of barbiturates or alcohol and from attempted suicide by hanging (Stromgren, 1946). Second, amnesia may be psychogenic; that is, it may develop for psychological rather than physiological reasons. The memory of the suicidal act, and of the desperate mood associated with it, may be so distressing to individuals that it is repressed and cannot be recalled voluntarily. In such cases, the subjects are not lying, but honestly cannot remember what happened. But whether failure to report deliberate drug ingestion is due to lying, somatogenic amnesia or psychogenic amnesia, it is by no means clearly attributable to drug automatism.

Alcohol consumption prior to suicide

Alcohol can be involved with suicidal behavior in a number of ways. Used prior to suicide, alcohol can ease a person's fear of death and give him the courage to kill himself. It can be taken together with medications to increase the lethality of the drugs. Alternatively, people who have been drinking without serious suicidal intent might impulsively kill themselves while intoxicated.

Used prior to suicide, alcohol can ease a person's fear of death and give him the courage to kill himself.

It has been found that a significant proportion of completed and attempted suicides drink alcohol prior to their suicidal actions. Welte's group (1988) found that 33 percent of a sample of completed suicides from Erie County, New York, had alcohol in their bloodstream. In a British study, Varadaraj and Mendonca (1987) found that 41 percent of a sample of attempted suicides were intoxicated.

Alcohol intoxication at the time of the suicidal act is more common in those who leave no suicide note, have made no prior attempts, use a firearm and kill themselves in the evening or at night, and in males 20 to 60 years of age (Welte et al., 1988). Among suicide attempters, those who are intoxicated make more lethal attempts. It is conceivable that those engaging in suicidal behavior when intoxicated are more reckless and impulsive and therefore more likely to die.

Because the use of alcohol and drugs is often associated with attempts to change unhappy moods, it is not surprising that they would be involved in suicidal behavior. Alcoholism and drug abuse are intrinsically self-destructive behaviors, and they are also associated with an increased risk of both completed and attempted suicide. Drugs, especially sedatives and antidepressants, are popular methods for suicide, and often despondent persons drink alcohol prior to their suicidal acts. Suicide in some cases has been attributed to a state known as "drug automatism" in which people overdose without serious suicidal intent, but there is little hard evidence for this phenomenon.

References

Aitken, R.C. and Proudfoot, A.T. Barbiturate automatism. *Postgraduate Medicine* 45:612–616, 1963.

Baker, S.P., O'Neill, B. and Karpf, R.S. *The Injury Fact Book*. Lexington, MA: D.C. Heath, 1984.

Beasley, C.M., Potvin, J.H., Masica, D.N., et al. Fluoxetine. *Journal of Affective Disorders* 24:1–10, 1992.

Clarke, R.V. and Lester, D. *Suicide: Closing the Exits*. New York: Springer-Verlag, 1989.

Leonard, B.E. Cost benefit analysis of tricyclic antidepressant overdose. In B.E. Leonard and S.W. Parker (eds.), *Current Approaches: Risk/Benefits of Antidepressants*. Southampton, UK: Duphar Laboratories, 1988.

Lester, D. Changes in the methods used for suicide in 16 countries from 1960 to 1980. *Acta Psychiatrica Scandinavica* 81:260–261, 1990.

Lester, D. Alcoholism and drug abuse. In R.W. Maris, A.L. Berman, J.T.

Maltsberger and R.I. Yufit (eds.), *Assessment and Prediction of Suicide.* New York: Guilford, 1992.

Lester, D. Controlling crime facilitators: Evidence from research on homicide and suicide. *Crime Prevention Studies* 1:35–54, 1993.

Litman, R.E., Shneidman, E.S., Farberow, N.L., et al. Investigations of equivocal suicides. *Journal of the American Medical Association* 184:924–929, 1963.

Menninger, K.A. *Man Against Himself.* New York: Harcourt, Brace & World, 1938.

National Committee for Injury Prevention and Control, "Injury Prevention: Meeting the Challenge," 1993.

Retterstol, N. *Suicide: A European Perspective.* New York: Cambridge University Press, 1993.

Roy, A. and Linnoila, M. Alcoholism and suicide. *Suicide and Life-Threatening Behavior* 16:244–273, 1986.

Stromgren, E. Mental sequelae of suicidal attempts by hanging. *Acta Psychiatrica* 21:753–780, 1946.

Varadaraj, R. and Mendonca, J. A survey of blood alcohol levels in self-poisoning cases. *Advances in Alcohol and Substance Abuse* 7(1):63–69, 1987.

Welte, J., Abel, E., and Wieczorek, W. The role of alcohol in suicides in Erie County, New York, 1972–1984. *Public Health Reports* 103:648–652, 1988.

8

Abortion Contributes to Teen Suicide

David C. Reardon

David C. Reardon is the director of the Elliot Institute, an organization that researches the effects of abortion on women, men, siblings, and society. He also serves as editor of the Post-Abortion Review, *a quarterly publication of the Elliot Institute.*

Research shows that women who are pregnant tend to have a lower suicide rate than women who are not pregnant, suggesting that pregnancy gives women something to live for. Conversely, studies have found that teenage girls and women who have abortions are more than ten times as likely to commit suicide than girls and women who have not had abortions. Post-abortion suicides are often the result of the mother's guilt feelings and despair over the death of the unborn child. When a woman confides that she is considering an abortion, her confidante must provide her with support and encouragement for preserving the life of her unborn child.

In the 1960s, when abortions were available only for "therapeutic" reasons, it was not uncommon for persons with the means and know-how to obtain an abortion on psychiatric grounds. In some states, all that was necessary was to find an agreeable psychiatrist willing to diagnose every woman with a problem pregnancy as "suicidal."

Yet all the studies done on this issue show that pregnancy is actually correlated with a dramatic *decreased* rate of suicide compared to non-pregnant women. This has led some psychiatrists to suggest that pregnancy somehow serves a psychologically protective role. The presence of another person to "live for" appears to reduce the suicidal impulses of a mentally disturbed or deeply depressed woman.[1]

The abortion-suicide link

Although pregnancy weakens suicidal impulses, there is strong evidence that abortion dramatically *increases* the risk of suicide. According to a

Reprinted from "The Abortion/Suicide Connection," by David C. Reardon, *Post-Abortion Review*, Summer 1993, with permission from the author.

1986 study by researchers at the University of Minnesota, a teenage girl is 10 times more likely to attempt suicide if she has had an abortion in the last six months than is a comparable teenage girl who has not had an abortion.[2] Other studies have found similar statistical significance between a history of abortion and suicide attempts among adults. Thus, the actual data suggests that abortion is far more likely to drive an unstable woman to suicide than is pregnancy and childbirth.

This abortion/suicide link is well known among professionals who counsel suicidal persons. For example, Meta Uchtman, director of the Cincinnati chapter of Suiciders Anonymous, reported that in a 35 month period her group worked with 4,000 women, of whom 1,800 or more had abortions. Of those who had abortions, 1,400 were between the ages of 15 and 24, the age group with the fastest growing suicide rate in the country.

Sometimes a post-abortion suicide attempt is an impulsive act of despair. For example, 18-year-old "Susan" writes: "Two days after the abortion I wrote a suicide note to my parents and boyfriend. I just couldn't fathom how I could possibly live with the knowledge of what I had done. I killed my own baby! I went down to the basement and figured out how to shoot my father's pistol. Hysterical and crying I put the barrel of the gun into my mouth. All of a sudden I heard someone upstairs. For some reason my father had stopped by to pick up something. I stopped what I was doing and went upstairs. He saw that I was upset and asked me if I wanted to have lunch with him at noon. I felt I at least owed him lunch. By the time lunch was over I was too scared to do it."

A teenage girl is 10 times more likely to attempt suicide if she has had an abortion in the last six months than is a comparable teenage girl who has not had an abortion.

Other times, the suicidal impulses result from years of repression, depression, and lost self-esteem. A 1987 study of women who suffered from post-abortion trauma found that 60 percent had experienced suicidal ideation, 28 percent had attempted suicide, and 18 percent had attempted suicide more than once, often several years after the event.[3]

Sadly, in at least one documented case, an 18-year-old committed suicide three days after having a suction abortion because of guilt feelings over having "killed her baby." Later examination of the clinic's records revealed that she had not actually been pregnant.

Perhaps one reason for the strong abortion/suicide link exists in the fact that in many ways abortion is like suicide. A person who threatens suicide is actually crying out for help. So are women who contemplate abortion. Both are in a state of despair. Both are lonely. Both feel faced by insurmountable odds.

Some "right-to-die" groups argue that we should legalize suicide and even create suicide clinics where facilitators would ease people through their suicide decisions. If we did so, there would be no shortage of desperate people willing to exercise their "freedom to choose." Promised a "quick, easy and painless" solution to their problems, suicide rates would skyrocket just as abortion rates did in the 1970s.

Like the suicide clinics described above, abortion clinics also exploit desperate people. They promise to release clients from the darkness of their despair. They appeal to our consumer society's demand for instant solutions to all our problems. They pose as places of compassion, but they are actually reaping huge profits through the harvest of the lonely, frightened, and confused people who are "unwanted" by society. In place of life, they offer the "compassion" of death.

Granting the wish for suicide or abortion is not an aid to desperate people. It is abandonment. It is a false compassion that protects us from getting entangled in the "personal problems" of others. It is "cheap love."

A cry for help

To those who look deeply, and care deeply, it is clear that people who express a desire for suicide or abortion are really crying out for help. They are crying out for the support and encouragement to choose life, cherish life, and rejoice in life. They are crying out for an infusion of hope.

Just as a suicidal person is crying out for help when she tells others she wishes she were dead, so a woman who is distressed over a pregnancy is crying out for help when she tells others she is considering abortion. In both cases, the desperate person is reaching out in the hope that someone will announce they truly care, and will truly help them. They need to see the value of life, their own as well as their child's, reflected in the love of those who would help them preserve that life. They need to hear that they are strong enough to triumph in the life that is theirs, and that whenever they grow weak, we will be there to strengthen them and even carry them.

This requires us to engage in "costly love," a love that demands a real sacrifice of time, energy, and resources. Anything less, they will interpret as "You don't really care." Anything less, and they will be right.

Notes

1. Hilgers, et al, *New Perspectives on Human Abortion* (Frederick, Md.: University Press of America, 1981) 156.

2. Garfinkel, et al., *Stress, Depression and Suicide: A Study of Adolescents in Minnesota* (Minneapolis: University of Minnesota Extension Service, 1986).

3. Reardon, "A Survey of Psychological Reactions," (Springfield, IL: Elliot Institute, 1987).

9

Many Factors Put Teens at Risk of Suicide

Lynn M. Tefft

Lynn M. Tefft is a staff writer for the Cedar Rapids, Iowa, Gazette.

Most teens who commit suicide lack a sense of hope and feel that suicide is the only way to stop their pain or end their troubles. Certain risk factors, such as substance abuse, impulsive behavior, a lack of decision-making skills, or an absence of close or supportive relationships, may heighten teens' feelings of hopelessness. Furthermore, the suicides of prominent figures lead some teens to believe that suicide will earn them the attention they crave.

At 4:20 p.m. Oct. 3, 1994, Marilyn McEnany's life changed forever. McEnany, of Marion [Iowa], came home from work to find her 17-year-old son, Scott, dead from carbon monoxide poisoning in his sport-utility vehicle. An eight-page suicide note lay near his body.

"When I went into that garage, I looked at his face and down to his feet and back up to his face and thought, 'How can he do this to me?'" McEnany says.

Scott was one of an estimated 5,350 people age 15 to 24 who committed suicide nationwide in 1994, according to statistics from the Centers for Disease Control and Prevention. In Iowa that year, 41 young people ages 10 to 19 took their own lives, according to the Iowa Department of Public Health.

A ripple effect

The suicide of a teen-ager creates a ripple effect of grief, anger and questions. Those left behind are bewildered and hurt, taking the blame and asking themselves what they could have done. Some are angry with the deceased for giving up and deserting them.

Marilyn and Thomas McEnany divorced after their son's death.

"We can go on the rest of our lives and we will question why he did it. No matter what you do, everything you relate to comes back to that.

Why did your kid do this?" says Thomas McEnany.

His son's note—detailing his perceived failure at life—offered some explanation but left his parents wondering why he didn't seek their help.

Each teen who commits suicide is wrestling with something that he or she can no longer live with, say counselors who work with depressed and suicidal teens.

Unfortunately, counselors say, there is no way to predict whether a teen-ager will commit suicide. However, they say, certain risk factors—lifestyles and behaviors—push some teen-agers toward it.

Risk factors know no geographic boundaries.

Constance Garrett, director of the Boys Town National Hotline based in Omaha, Nebraska, says, "I take calls from all over the country. The problems kids are facing in Iowa City and New York City are very similar."

Psychologists, social workers and school counselors say teens commit suicide for the same reason adults do—a lack of hope.

Says Stephen Trefz, a social worker with the Mid-Eastern Iowa Community Mental Health Center in Iowa City, "They're seeing suicide as a viable option to reducing some real emotional pain."

Counselors say these teens feel they're out of options—they're too emotionally exhausted to look for other solutions.

"I think it's very difficult for adults to think a 13-year-old can get that hopeless," says Elizabeth Lilly, a social worker at the Family Counseling Center of St. Luke's Hospital in Cedar Rapids [Iowa].

Risk factors

Certain risk factors, such as substance abuse and a lack of supportive family members or friends, can make some of them more prone to this sense of hopelessness, counselors say.

Some risk factors seem obvious. Others, like lack of decision-making skills, are more subtle. Few are unique to teenagers; most apply to adults and teens alike.

What of simply being a teen-ager? Sam Cochran of the University of Iowa Counseling Service notes that for some, adolescence is a time to experiment with different lifestyles and risky behaviors.

Adolescents may have difficulty grasping the gravity of suicide—the impact of succeeding.

"They're not reckoning with death," Cochran says. "When they commit suicide, it's to solve a problem or get back at someone. For us, suicide is the end as we know it. That's not quite so obvious to some young people."

Not surprisingly, teen-agers who have a history of starting and quickly quitting activities—scouting, baseball, school, for example—may be at risk for suicide, counselors say.

They say a family history of suicide is another red flag. The same goes for families with a history of depression. Teens in these family situations may not be more likely to commit suicide, but they are more apt to consider it as an option.

Others at high risk are those dealing with substance abuse by a family member or abusing drugs themselves. Teens who turn to drugs or alcohol are sometimes victims of a cruel irony. They believe the drugs or alcohol will ease their problems, when in fact the substances can make them more depressed and hopeless.

"I haven't seen many truly suicidal kids who haven't been affected by alcohol or drug usage, either within their group, their family or within themselves," says Steve Schwet, a counselor at Linn-Mar High School [in Marion] since 1981.

Don Lyness, a counselor at West Delaware High School [in Manchester, Iowa] for three years and a counselor at North Linn High School for 15 years before that, sees it differently.

Teens commit suicide for the same reason adults do—a lack of hope.

"I don't think that it's one of the factors you can say is almost always present in situations like that," he says. "I think I've probably had just as many really depressed students who were serious about suicide who really weren't using at all and just as many on the other side, too."

A somewhat more subtle risk is lack of a support network.

Teens in this situation don't have close family relationships, perhaps because they're being abused or simply because no one seems to have time for them. They don't have friends to fill that void, either, counselors say.

These teens keep their problems to themselves. They might seem OK, but the problems are festering. No one is there to help the teen separate the rational thoughts from the irrational ones.

"I'm always concerned about the student who may be a loner, a student who doesn't really have any friends," says Lyness.

Particularly isolated are teens dealing with homosexuality. Statistics show gay teen-agers commit an estimated 30 percent of teen suicides. Counselors say some gay teen-agers are not supported by their families and have to lie to themselves and to other people, or face scorn if they tell the truth.

Teens who feel they don't have anywhere to vent their frustrations, anger and problems also may not have people from whom to learn coping skills, counselors say.

Peg Schollmeier, a counselor at West High School in Iowa City, says teens without coping skills tend to overreact to negative events.

"I don't mean that as a criticism, but they never really have learned to deal with situations and react very strongly to what we might consider very minor situations," she says.

St. Luke's Lilly calls it rigidity, a view of life that confines solutions to problems to just one—it's one way or no way.

Media influence

People looking for someone or something to blame for teen suicide may point their fingers at songs that focus on suicide, such as Ozzy Osbourne's "Suicide Solution" and Garbage's "No. 1 Crush." And they may blame movies that might seem to glorify the act—"Dead Poets Society" and "Heathers," for example.

But those themes are likely to affect only those teens already unable to cope with their problems, counselors say.

What can have more of an effect is the suicide of public figures like Kurt Cobain, the Nirvana lead singer who shot himself in 1994. Cobain received as much publicity in death as he did in life. Counselors say teens craving attention may see suicide as a quick way to get it.

"They think, 'Look at all the recognition I get,'" says UI's Cochran. "But you don't get that—you're dead."

One not-so-obvious media influence is the Internet. A simple search for the word "suicide" yields Web pages trumpeting the glory of suicide and providing how-tos in a variety of methods.

Pressures on teens

Eastern Iowa teens say they understand how the pressures of life can become overwhelming. They cite a wide range of pressures, from excelling in athletics to starting romantic relationships. They may be looking to get into good colleges. They are trying to balance the demands of their parents with those of their friends. They are struggling to define themselves.

"All the school activities—you have to find a way to balance all of it," says Angie Ehlers, 16, a West Delaware High School student who lives in Stanley.

Adds Lori Rich, a 16-year-old Mid-Prairie High School student from Kalona [Iowa], "You have to do everything in high school but you don't have time. It wears you down."

These pressures can become particularly intense for teens who are perfectionists.

"They have to do everything and be the best at everything," West High's Schollmeier says. "They just get to that point where they're overwhelmed."

In his suicide note, Scott McEnany told his parents he didn't feel he would ever be as good as his brother and sister were.

"Like in school he wasn't as smart as they were. He felt like a loser," says Marilyn McEnany. "He wanted us to [be] proud of him like we were so proud of the other two."

No matter whether there's a suicide note explaining the reason, or a psychologist speculating on the reason, it's never enough for those left behind. To them there's no reason to just give up.

"It's your job as a parent to keep your child safe and you didn't do that," says Bonnie Tindal of Kalona, whose 15-year-old daughter, Laura, shot herself on April 6, 1993. "So that stays with you forever."

10

The Extent of Teen Suicide Is Exaggerated

Mike Males

Mike Males is the author of The Scapegoat Generation: America's War on Adolescents.

Teenagers have the second lowest suicide rate of any age group; only the rate for preteens is lower. In addition, teen suicide rates in the 1990s are not the highest in U.S. history. The perception that teen suicide has been rising is due to the increase in accurate reporting procedures. Often ruled as "accidents" in the past, many teen deaths are now labeled correctly as suicides. Furthermore, statistics concerning failed suicide attempts are highly suspect. Most failed teen suicide attempts are not true efforts to die, but bids for attention. The patterns, methods, and circumstances in which teens kill themselves closely mirror those of adults of the same gender, era, and background.

The most dramatic assertion for the allegedly rising self-destruction of modem teens is the claim that the rate of teen suicide has quadrupled since 1950, including a doubling since 1970.[1] Suicide is a pure indicator of high risk behavior, of self-destructive intent. By definition, suicide is always self-inflicted, always fatal, contains no element of mere "bad luck," inexperience, or "being in the wrong place at the wrong time," and is the only crime for which the characteristics of the victim are identical to those of the perpetrator.

Even if taken at face value, the scary-sounding claim of "epidemic" teen suicide amounts to a lot less when a never-mentioned fact (easily seen in the tables) is considered: For both sexes and all races, teenagers experience the *lowest* suicide rates of any age group except pre-teens.[2] In 1992, about 1 in 12,000 teens ages 13–19 committed suicide, compared to 1 in 6,000 young and middle-aged adults and 1 in 5,000 older adults. If suicide were adopted as the standard, teenagers would be judged uniquely immune to self-destruction.

A quadrupling in teen suicide since 1950 would represent a change in behavior by approximately 1 in 10,000 teens age 15–19. That is far from a widespread trend sufficient to support the kinds of dire assertions about adolescent mental health that have accompanied it. Further, as will be seen, it is unlikely that teen suicide has increased as claimed.

Puzzlement over why a few teenagers—about one in a sizeable high school of 2,000 students every five or six years—commit suicide has become mired in just such generalized speculations about the mental health of adolescents. When suicidal teens are studied directly, some clear differences emerge. These are not "average" youths. The reasons for their suicidal feelings often are not comfortable for adults to contemplate.

Figure 1: U.S. teen and adult violent death trends are similar over time

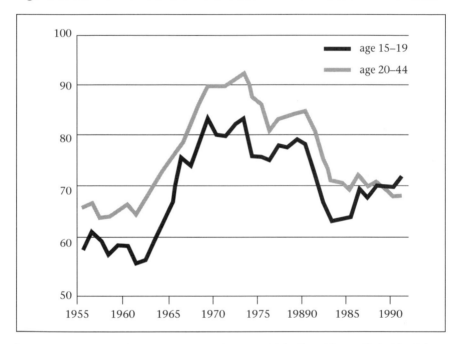

Source: National Center of Health (annual) Vital Statistics of the United States, 1955–1991. Volume II, Part A, Mortality. Washington, DC: U.S. Department of Health and Human Services. See Table 2.

One of the biggest is a history of sexual abuse. In a 1992 study of 276 low-income pregnant teenagers, a California pediatrics team found histories of physical and sexual abuse increased the risk of suicide four-fold.[3] Similarly, a 1993 survey of 5,000 exemplars by Who's Who Among American High School Students found that the one in seven girls who had been sexually assaulted were four times more likely to have attempted suicide (17 percent versus 4 percent) than students who had not been assaulted.[4] The 1992 *Rape in America* study of 4,000 women found one-third of rape victims had contemplated suicide and that 13 percent had attempted suicide. In contrast, suicide attempts were practically non-existent (only 1 percent reported having tried) among females who had not been raped. Of those raped, 62 percent had been victimized prior to age 18.[5]

In addition to sexual abuse, key factors in suicide incidence are maleness, homosexuality, economic stress, childhood neglect and violence, and individual biochemistry.[6] Most of these factors cannot be changed by the affected individual, but they can be changed by changes in social environments and attitudes. For example, child abuse and neglect and negative attitudes toward homosexuality can be addressed by changes in policies and attitudes controlled by adults.

Table 1: Teens are not the age group most likely to die from violence

Deaths per 100,000 population by age, race, and sex, 1991							
All races	*10–14*	*15–19*	*20–24*	*25–29*	*30–34*	*35–39*	*40–44*	*45–49*
All deaths	25.8	89.0	110.1	123.0	154.1	197.7	253.6	380.5
All violent deaths	14.7	71.8	84.2	71.6	67.2	61.1	54.6	54.2
Males	20.6	108.6	134.8	114.2	107.9	95.2	84.7	81.4
Females	8.6	32.9	31.7	28.7	28.7	27.5	25.1	28.0
White	9.9	58.7	69.9	57.3	57.1	54.7	51.0	50.8
Hispanic	17.7	83.6	87.4	82.0	76.2	68.5	58.7	53.6
Black	22.8	115.3	160.7	136.8	126.0	115.6	106.6	87.5
Asian/other	5.0	23.0	26.0	25.7	24.6	23.7	23.3	24.9
All accidents	11.1	41.2	44.4	36.6	35.3	32.9	30.3	29.4
Auto accidents	6.1	31.2	32.8	23.3	19.3	16.2	14.2	14.6
All other acc.	4.8	9.1	10.7	12.1	14.3	14.8	14.6	13.7
Suicide	1.4	11.0	14.9	14.9	15.5	15.1	14.3	15.7
Homicide	2.2	19.6	25.0	20.1	16.4	13.1	10.0	9.1

Source: National Center for Health Statistics (1995). *Vital Statistics of the United States* 1991. Mortality, Part B. Washington, DC: U.S. Department of Health and Human Services, Table 8-5. Hispanic and white totals apportioned from 1990 national and California ethnicity breakdowns.

These changes are not easy to accomplish and require sacrifices and long-term commitments harder to bring about than mere quick-fix salvos aimed at "teen suicide." Former Secretary of Health and Human Services Louis Sullivan, illustrating how political prejudices remain part of the nation's health problem, repudiated a portion of a January 1989 HHS report urging a more positive stance toward homosexuality as a way of reducing high suicide rates among gay youth, drawing criticism from the American Psychological Association and the American Association of Suicidology.[7]

As on other troubling issues, federal health authorities have avoided unsettling questions and instead have lent the impression that suicide means there is just something wrong with teenagers. A 1995 CDC report stated that suicide among 10–14-year-olds has "soared" since 1980. When the numbers were examined, the "soaring" consisted of the fact that 1 in

60,000 youths age 10–14 committed suicide in 1992, compared to 1 in 125,000 in 1980. Nor did the CDC mention that the most recent suicide figures show 10–14-year-olds are only one-tenth as likely to commit suicide as are adults.[8] The report blamed gun availability, childhood drug abuse, aggression, family problems (which authorities typically blame on unstable youths), and stress. The image of teen suicide as a technical challenge, curable by legal adjustments, programs, and treatments aimed at youths continues to be the official-recommended diagnosis and remedy.[9]

Perceptions of youth suicide and its causes seem to depend on prevailing beliefs about the young, death, the state of society. Teenage suicide, like adult suicide, was almost certainly higher in a number of past eras in the United States than today—the most recent being the early 1900s, the Depression years, and the early 1970s. Today's is not America's first wave of panic over the young taking their own lives. Nor has our understanding of youth suicide advanced much over that of eighty years ago, when assertions of "epidemic child suicide" gripped Europe, Russia, and the United States.

Teen suicide, 1920: Feminism and moral decay

American authorities, even in an era when many states did not report deaths to the Bureau of the Census registry, found a rapidly rising rate of youths taking their own lives. In 1915, there were 395 youth suicides reported among the two-thirds of all reporting states, leading to an estimate of 600 for the entire nation.[10] Three thousand additional teenage deaths from firearms, poisonings, and drownings (all leading methods of suicide) were ruled as "accidents" that year. The media described the toll as "staggering." Famed Stanford University child psychologist Lewis Terman lamented:

> Suicides, like all forms of crime, are becoming more and more precocious. In these days children leave their marbles and tops to commit suicide, tired of life almost before they have tasted it.[11]

"Nothing should cause more real alarm than the suicide of children," the newly formed Save-a-Life League declared in 1920, noting that teen suicides were projected at 100 more than in 1919. The "appalling rate of child suicide," wrote *Literary Digest's* editors in 1921, "is a frightful indictment of our Christian civilization . . . the average age of boys is sixteen years and girls fifteen."[12]

Based on European rates and rates among American adults, Terman estimated the true level of youth suicide in early 20th century America at 2,000 per year—if accurate, a rate double that of today. "The official [suicide] figures are certainly below the actual facts, because of the well-known tendency of relatives to assign the cause of death to accident," Terman wrote. Just as today, it was not clear that teen suicides were rising so much as being better reported and distinguished from fatal accidents, perhaps even exaggerated. Just as today, the detail that a youth suicide epidemic might not exist did not stop pundits of 1920 from citing the "youth suicide epidemic" as proof of whatever evil the commentator most deplored.

The *Catholic Universe* blamed utilitarianism, "refined paganism," and a production-obsessed society. "Our children are not so clean and innocent as those of an earlier generation," the church contended. "The men and women of to-day [1921] have not the moral strength of their ancestors."[13] The *Baltimore American* blamed feminists' "steadily insidious propaganda to stir up hostility between the sexes" for pressuring young women to assert their "superiority." Young women were committing suicide in record numbers in despair of Suffragette messages that "they were the coming mistresses of civilization; men were back numbers; marriage was a relation of convenience; the world had been made a mess by the ignoramuses now in control."[14]

Table 2: How statistics manufacture an epidemic: Teen girls' suicides are plummeting, boys' suicides skyrocketing?

U.S. teen deaths, 1915*	*Males 10–19*	*Females 10–19*
Total firearms and poisoning deaths	661	279
Ruled as suicides	126	160
Percent ruled suicide	19%	57%
Firearms/poisoning deaths/100,000 teens	10.2	4.3
Total suicides/100,000 teens	2.7	3.4
U.S. teen deaths, 1990		
Total firearms and poisoning deaths	2,058	420
Ruled as suicides	1,394	311
Percent ruled suicide	68%	74%
Firearms/poisoning deaths/100,000 teens	11.5	2.5
Total suicide rate/100,000 teens	10.3	2.3
Change, 1915–1990		
Firearms/poisoning deaths/100,000 teens	+12.7%	–41.9%
Total suicide rate/100,000 teens	+281.5%	–32.4%

*Death registration area covered 67.5 percent of U.S. population.

Sources: National Center for Health Statistics (1995). *Vital Statistics of the United States* 1990. Mortality, Part A. Washington, DC: U.S. Department of Health and Human Services, Table 1-27; U.S. Bureau of the Census (1915). *Mortality Statistics*. Washington, DC: U.S. Department of Commerce, Table 7.

Terman cited severe schooling, parental harshness, family disgraces, excessive ambitions placed on the young, "cheap theatres, pessimistic literature, sensational stories, the newspaper publicity given to crime and suicides, and the dangerous suggestive effect of the suicide of relatives or comrades—in other words, contagion, in the broad sense," as well as alcoholism, venereal disease, heredity, illegitimacy, divorce, and just plain "morbid impulse." Although schools were blamed for rising youth suicide, "education may make just the difference" in suicide prevention as well, he added.[15]

Divorce, congested living conditions, and Prohibition (apparently some youth were thought to prefer death to drought) were accused by various sources. High suicide rates were also found among those of "wealth and social position," the League observed. Noting that boys most often used guns, and girls poison, just as today, the League (eight decades before the CDC) called for "strictly enforced laws to suppress the sale of all poisons and firearms."[16]

Another panic ensued in 1927 when a "wave of suicides" was reported among college students. Terms such as "terrifying" and "epidemic" were common in the popular press again, along with contention that rising cynicism and materialism among youth were at fault.[17] However, in 1932, Arthur Beeley of the University of Utah presented figures showing that although there had been great publicity attached to the suicides of 26 students from prominent families, there had been no unusual rise in youth suicides that year. "Writers who assumed the alleged 'wave' to be fact and understood to point out its causes and suggest a cure" for the "epidemic" contributed to the hysteria, Beeley declared.[18] But on it marched. In 1937, *Science News Letter* reported that kids "as young as six to 13" were being treated in hospitals for suicide attempts and preoccupation with death.[19]

Examining teenage suicide trends in historical context produces an astonishing fact: Certified suicide rates among teenage girls are 30 percent *lower* in the 1990s than in 1915, while suicide rates among teenage boys are alleged to have risen fourfold! Coroners of 1915 were particularly inclined to find deliberate intent in firearms and poisoning deaths among teenage girls, ruling 57 percent as suicides—three times more than among boys (Table 2).

Note that the overall teenage death rate from firearms and poisonings is virtually the same today as it was 75 years ago. Note also that fatality rates from these mostly self-inflicted deaths, including suicides, have dropped considerably for girls. What has changed is that the *proportion* of male deaths ruled as suicides has risen dramatically. The official judgment of suicidal intentions of boy-mind versus girl-mind has arrived at a bizarre kind of gender equality. It is not that more boys are dying, but that their deaths are much more likely to be classified as suicides today.

To take literally the past records of teen suicide is to introduce anomaly after anomaly. Such rulings appear to have as much to do with prevailing public and coroner attitudes and prejudices toward the age, sex, and race of the deceased, and their assumed generic tendencies to "suicides" or "accidents," than to consistent analysis of the circumstances of similar types of death. Commentators of the first four decades of the 1900s left little more to be said, shouted, blamed, pushed, or debunked on the subject of teenage suicide.

Today's teen suicides vs. yesterday's "accidents"

On February 8, 1953, the Associated Press reported that the self-inflicted gunshot death of a 12-year-old New Jersey boy, originally ruled an accident, was re-certified as a suicide when a note was found in his pocket on the way to the cemetery. Coroners of 1953 were not inclined to rule deaths of 12-year-olds, even when self-inflicted under suspicious circumstances, as suicides. Fewer than a dozen were so classified that year. Only about 180 teenage firearms deaths in the whole country were labeled as suicides. Coroners often refused to do so unless there were suicide notes.

A 1957 study reported that notes were found in only 15 percent of all suicides. "Many committed suicides go unreported" due to "evasion, denial, concealment, and even direct suppression of evidence (such as relatives deliberately destroying suicide notes)," it found.[20] However, adults in that era were willing to believe teenagers could have fatal accidents. In 1953, some 650 teenagers died from mostly self-inflicted gunshot "accidents," one-third of the nation's firearms accident toll and a rate double that of adults. Even this "accident" level was an improvement over the 1930s, when teens accounted for nearly 40 percent of all accidental firearms mortality.

We move ahead 37 years to the most recent for which comprehensive figures are available, 1990. That year, in a youth population double that of 1953's, 1,474 teenage firearms deaths were classed as suicides—an apparent 500 percent increase in the rate. But only 520 firearms deaths among teens were ruled accidents or undetermined—a decrease of 65 percent. The overall teenage firearms mortality rate was little higher in 1990 than in 1953; only the way deaths were ruled had changed.

For both sexes and all races, teenagers experience the lowest *suicide rates of any age group except preteens.*

The supposed "increase" in teen suicide largely boils down to changes in the classification of firearms deaths among teenage boys. Prior to around 1960, fewer than one in five firearms deaths among teenage boys were classified as suicides. After 1960, this percentage steadily rose, so that by 1986 three-fourths of all firearms deaths among teenage boys were ruled suicides. This shift in firearms death classifications among boys accounts for three-fourths of the purported "rise" in teen suicide. No one has offered explanation as to why teenage boys should, in a 30-year period, become radically more suicide-prone and radically less accident-prone with firearms than was any other age group with any other instrument. The official theory that "gun availability" is to blame for teenage deaths does not explain such a large decrease in gunshot accidents. Since the decrease in adolescent firearms accidents did not serve any official theory, it—like other important youth behaviors—was simply ignored.

A few experts, most notably epidemiologist Paul Holinger in 1979, raised the question of whether a "selective certification artifact" might be lending the appearance of a rising teen suicide rate not occurring in reality.[21] In 1989, a study by Richard Gist and Q.B. Welch of the Kansas City Health Department documented the correspondence between the "rise" in teen "suicides" and the "fall" in teen "accidents."

Gist and Welch argued that the artifact of death certification changes are "the primary factor influencing suicide rates" among teenagers from firearms from 1955 through 1966, and that certification changes continued to influence reported teen suicide rates from 1967 through 1979. A large share of the apparent increase in teen suicide results, they argued, from increased willingness to certify equivocal teen firearms deaths as suicides and a corresponding "strongly consistent" decline in certifications

of such deaths as accidents. In particular, "youthful suicides may historically have been subject to greater levels of misreporting."[22] By the time
Gist and Welch first provided empirical evidence of a "primarily artifac-
tual epidemic" of teen suicide, publicity over its "skyrocketing" rate had
been raging for a decade.

Yet anomalies stood out everywhere. If suicides among teenagers increased both significantly and uniquely over the past 35 years, we would
expect to see a sharp rise in total (suicide + accident + undetermined)
deaths from firearms and poisonings not shared by other age groups. My
historical analysis of death tabulations by age from *Vital Statistics of the
United States* shows this is not the case.[23]

Figure 2 shows the trends for teenagers age 15–19 versus adults age
20–44 from 1953 to 1990 for certified suicides plus those types of mostly
self-inflicted "accidental" deaths (firearms and poisonings) most likely to be
ruled suicides. The trends are parallel, with adult death rates substantially
higher than those of teenagers. This close similarity in overall self-inflicted
death trends over time between the two age groups argues strongly that
there has been no unique increase in adolescent self-destruction.[24]

As Figure 2 shows, for both teens and adults, total deaths from firearms and poisonings, suicides and accidents (excluding homicides) were
stable from the 1950s to the early 1960s, rose sharply during the mid- and
late 1960s, peaked during the early 1970s, and declined slightly through
the 1980s. But while certified suicides comprise a consistent proportion

Figure 2: Teen and adult suicide/self-inflicted death trends are parallel

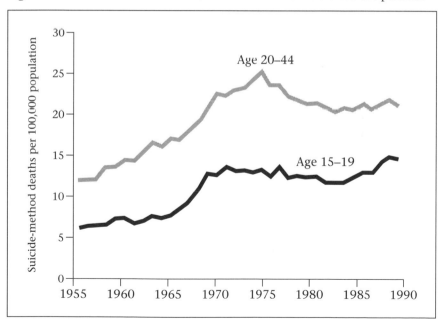

Source: National Center for Health Statistics. *Vital Statistics of the United States,* 1995–91. See Figure
1 and Table 3.

of total firearms-poisoning deaths for 20–44-year-olds for the entire period, certified suicides comprise a steadily rising (and certified accidents a
steadily falling) proportion of total firearms-poisoning deaths for 15–19-
year-olds.

The result, if the official view of rising teen suicide is valid, is that
from 1970 to 1990, the rate of teen suicide *rose* by 50 percent while the
overall rate of deaths from the two causes, which account for three-
fourths of all teen suicides, *decreased* by 60 percent. This implausibly large
decrease in teen accidental deaths from firearms and poisonings in just 20
years—which occurred among no other age groups and within no accident categories not connected with suicide—would be required to account for the above "suicide increase." If true, it would be an equally dramatic counter-trend!

Table 3: Teens are much less likely than adults to commit suicide

U.S. suicides per 100,000 persons of each age group, sex, and race, 1991					
Age group	*Total*	*Male*	*Female*	*White*	*Nonwhite*
10–14	1.5	2.3	0.7	1.6	1.0
15–19	11.0	17.6	3.7	11.8	7.8
All 10–19	6.2	10.0	2.2	6.7	4.4
20–24	14.9	25.4	3.9	13.6	11.3
25–34	15.2	25.0	5.4	16.0	11.3
35–44	14.7	24.0	6.5	15.9	8.1
All 20–44	14.9	24.7	5.5	15.5	9.9
45–64	15.5	24.4	7.1	16.6	7.9
Over 65	19.7	40.2	6.0	21.0	8.4
All ages >10	14.4	23.9	5.6	15.5	8.4

Source: National Center for Health Statistics (1995). *Vital Statistics of the United States* 1991. Mortality,
Volume I, Part B. Washington, DC: U.S. Department of Health and Human Services, Table 8-5.

Evidence of artifact is indicated in another area as well. In 1969, coroners ruled 434 deaths among teens age 15–19, including 300 firearms and
poisoning deaths, as "undetermined whether accidentally or purposely
inflicted." This number was equivalent to more than 40 percent of the
teen suicide toll that year. In 1987, only 149 teen deaths were ruled as
undetermined as to intent, including only 97 firearms and poisoning
deaths—a number equivalent to only 8 percent of the teen suicide toll.
The evidence is compelling: Coroners are becoming more adept at distinguishing teenage suicides from teenage self-inflicted "accidents."

The results of this analysis indicate three apparent facts:

(a) A significant past undercount of youth suicides is likely,

(b) Whatever change in youth suicide has occurred is not unique but
    a trend shared with adults, and

(c) Any youth suicide increase that did occur took place prior to 1972 and is not a modern phenomenon.

Yet agencies and official panels continue to overlook the certification question. In 1989, the Secretary of Health and Human Services' Task Force on Youth Suicide summarized the issue in its most inflammatory terms:

> The suicide rate for young people between ages 15 and 24 almost tripled during the past 30 years. . . . The sharp increase in suicide rates in one segment of the population, especially when most other causes of death were decreasing in the United States . . . has critical implications for public health priorities.[25]

So enrutted is the nature of youth suicide analysis that authorities do not consider any alternative explanations—especially as indicated by the closely parallel nature of trends in similar types of teen and adult deaths (the example highly relevant to suicide is shown in Figure 2) and the "seesaw" nature of teenage deaths ruled as accidents and as suicides in recent decades.

Worse still, Centers for Disease Control officials suggest that the true number of teen suicides could be double that now certified. This claim has been convincingly refuted by the Florida State University's Gary Kleck.[26] The only way the teen suicide rate could be higher is if the teen accidental death rate was lower—where else would the extra suicides come from? But if the teen suicide rate is twice as high, there would be very few deaths left over to classify as fatal accidents! Authorities would then have to explain why modern teenagers do not have fatal "accidents," while adults do. (Or at least, they would have to explain it among themselves, for such a surprising elimination of teenage accidents would not be discussed publicly until some major interest could be trotted out to take credit for it).

In many measures, statistics of the past are not reliably comparable to those of the present. Suicide certification—a definitive judgment demanding rigorous evidence as to perpetrator intent when the perpetrator is no longer around to question—requires complex investigation dependent upon coroner technique, training, and attitude. Most people who commit suicide do not leave notes. The question of whether today's teen suicide "epidemic" is not a real trend, but largely an artifact of improvement in the death classification process and awareness, is one that should have been thoroughly examined and disposed of before dire alarms were sent out to the public about unprecedented and terrifying adolescent self-annihilation.

Questioning the teenage "death wish"

The alarm among parents, professionals, schools, and youths themselves regarding the reported, inexplicably mushrooming incidence of young people taking their own lives has raised questions about adolescent mental health and led to extensive interventions aimed at stopping their purported self-destruction. The Centers for Disease Control's 1986 *Youth Suicide Surveillance* is characteristic, stating that, "in the past 30 years, the suicide rate among youth of the United States has increased dramati-

cally," with 15–24-year-olds said to represent "a high risk group" for suicide. Youth suicide has risen sharply "while the rate for the remainder of
the population remained stable," the C.D.C. states.[27] These assertions are
so common that few realize their dubious nature.

Teen suicide is considerably rarer than adult suicide. As Table 3 indicates, the puzzling aspect of suicide is not its teenage incidence, but its
high rate among young and middle-aged white male adults, who should
be experiencing a time of greatest opportunity.

---

*Teenage suicide, like adult suicide, was almost
certainly higher in a number of past eras in the
United States than today.*

Like other youth behaviors, suicide is patterned after cultural norms.
Adult men age 20–44 commit suicide 4.5 times more than women that
age; teenage boys commit suicide 4.5 times more than teenage girls.
Young and middle-aged white adults are 1.6 times more likely to kill
themselves than corresponding nonwhite adults, and white teens are 1.5
times more suicidal than nonwhite teens.

Massachusetts and Alaska, respectively, consistently display the nation's lowest and highest adult suicide rates, and also the nation's lowest
and highest teen suicide rates. In 1990, firearms, poisons, and hangings
accounted for 61 percent, 18 percent, and 10 percent of all adult suicides,
respectively; and 66 percent, 10 percent, and 21 percent of all teen suicides. Women's suicides are five times more likely to involve drug overdoses than men's suicides; and teenage girls' suicides are seven times
more likely to involve drug overdoses than those of teenage boys.

Homosexuals account for an estimated one-third of all adult suicides,
and 30 percent of all adolescent suicides. Youths whose parent committed suicide are several times more likely to commit suicide themselves.[28]
Despite correlations so consistent they can only be called overwhelming,
links between youth and adult suicide are rarely mentioned in the scientific literature and never in media treatments of the "epidemic."

As with the case of drunken driving and drug abuse, when teenage behaviors turn out to be less alarming in reality than officials and program-
mers want to depict, the measures are changed. It has become standard
for psychiatric lobbies (as shown later) and agencies to lump the much
higher suicide tolls among 20–24-year-olds with those of teens, produce
a total of "5,000 to 6,000 per year," and then label this exaggerated number as "teenage suicides"—a figure popular in the media as well.[29] And
rather than talk about the comparatively low teenage suicide death toll,
most discussions of teen suicide have switched the measure to much
murkier and uninterpretable self-reported behaviors such as self-reported
"suicide ideation" or "suicide attempts."

Questioning teen suicide "attempts" and "contagion"

The punk band Suicidal Tendencies rants in "Suicidal Failure" (in which
the inept narrator employs guns, pills, jumping off a bridge, lye, hanging,

heroin overdose, driving off a cliff, and poison: "BUT I'M STILL NOT DEAD!") that the human body can prove difficult to dispatch. Still, suicide is a deliberate and calculated act. We would not expect that a truly suicide-bound individual would accidentally survive many attempts given the efficacy of readily available instruments. I recalled four teenage suicides I had reported on in my ten years as a Bozeman, Montana, journalist. Three shootings and one hanging from one girl and three boys ages 13, 14, 17, and 18—no ambivalence, no ineptness, no failures on their part.

Yet we are told by health officials and psychiatric authorities that hundreds of thousands, even millions, of teenagers "attempt suicide" every year but somehow don't die. The CDC estimates that about 3.5 million 9–12 grade students have "suicide ideation," 2 million have made "specific suicide plans," and over 1 million have made "suicide attempts."[30] Other self-reporting surveys estimate 500,000 teenage "suicide attempts" every year ("one every minute of every day," in the language of today's hype). As in the case of eighth grade boys' reports of sexual achievement, experts have taken these reports of adolescent "suicide ideation," "suicide plans," and "suicide attempts" at face value, which is manifestly silly, rather than considering the alternatives.

The supposed "increase" in teen suicide largely boils down to changes in the classification of firearms deaths among teenage boys.

For example, is it possible that what is being reported are thoughts such as the following 14-year-old's?

> It seemed to him that life was but a trouble, at best. . . . It must be very peaceful, he thought, to lie and slumber and dream forever and ever, with the wind whispering through the trees and caressing the grass and the flowers over the grave, and nothing to bother and grieve about, ever any more. If he only had a clean Sunday-school record, he could be willing to go, and be done with it all.

If Hannibal, Missouri, of Mark Twain times had self-reporting surveys, thoughts like those would have scored ideation, perhaps even plans. Yet Tom Sawyer hardly seems the profile of the suicidal teen. Is it possible that "suicide attempts," particularly given the fact that these are so disproportionately found among sexually abused girls, are efforts to get attention and help from a previously oblivious adult society?

In 1987, a week after the suicide of a popular 13-year-old girl in a Montana mountain town, I interviewed a dozen of her best friends, ages 13–15, alone and for an hour or more each, on their thoughts of suicide. All "said they had seriously contemplated suicide at one time or another in their lives. All said they are no longer considering the idea now." Perhaps their elaborations illuminate what adolescents mean by the boxes they check on self-reporting surveys.

Suicide ideation:

"I could get away from my problems. I wouldn't have to change the sheets or do my homework," an eighth grade girl said. "It's like a video game—you die, you're out of the game, the problem is over. You get to start again.

"But now I think, 'You die, but your problems are still there. Killing yourself is like staying in a hole forever.'"

. . ."Yes, I thought seriously about killing myself," another 14-year-old said, poking moodily at a sandwich in her kitchen. "I didn't wear clean clothes, my bedroom wasn't clean, I had a poor self-image. I didn't think I was popular."

Plans:

"Once I thought about killing myself when I was really up-set about the way people were treating me," another 14-year-old said, sitting in her living room and scribbling ab-sently in a notebook.

Memories of being sexually abused when she was younger kept "popping up in my mind," the girl said.

"I thought about taking pills or cutting my wrists. But my friends talked me out of it," she said.

. . ."I talked to them, and the problem began to go away. If I killed myself, my mom and my friends would take it very hard. It's not the easiest way out, it's the hardest way."

An attempt:

"I tried to kill myself when I was thirteen, but mainly I wanted attention," a girl said, chewing on a taco at a fast-food restaurant.

"I wanted people to notice me. I wanted my mom to look at me. She was really sleeping around with everybody then, a regular town whore.

"I got a razor and made a cut on my wrist in the bathroom. I was really upset that day. I got attention, all right.

"My best friend came in the bathroom and saw the blood and started screaming.

"I started thinking, 'My dad really loves me, my sister looks up to me, plus if I don't stay around, my best friend will wind up going out with some sleazebag.'

"And plus I thought, 'Wait a minute, this hurts.'"

In none of the hours-long interviews with these distressed eighth and ninth graders, a week after one of their closest friends shot herself with a .357 magnum, did I encounter the purported illusions of invulnerability, lack of appreciation of the finality of death, self-preoccupation, or glamorizing of suicide that authorities so often attribute to adolescents.

What I found instead was a biting realism. "Suicide is stupid, idiotic," said one 15-year-old of her best friend's demise. "You only really get that attention for a day. Then it starts to fade away." "What she did was wrong," another told me. "She hurt us a lot." What the dead cheerleader candidate's friends did the night after her death would send experts into apoplexy. They acquired a copious supply of alcohol and pot, sat up the night together in an empty house talking about their friend and suicide—and made a pact with each other to talk more openly about their despair.

"Lots of kids see no hope for the future, but we're not going to do that [kill ourselves]," one eighth grader told me. Another 14-year-old summed up the wake: "You've got to talk about your problems, not let them eat and eat and eat at you. If she had, she wouldn't be dead."[31] If more sane attitudes toward suicide have been articulated, I haven't encountered them.

How can experts get this so wrong? If 500,000 teens attempt suicide annually, and only 2,000 succeed, this represents an astonishing failure rate of 250 to one. Modern girls (considered the scheming sex in 1915) must be especially inept. While 10 percent of teen females are reported to have attempted suicide, only one in every 5,000 girls actually kills herself during her entire adolescence through age 19. That's 500 failed attempts for every suicide.

Either suicidal adolescents are a lot stupider than we think, the methods at hand are not really that deadly, or these are not true "suicide attempts." A "suicide attempt" is a deliberate effort to die. It fails only due to unanticipated inadequacy of the method or intervention of a rescuer. The tendency of adolescents (and to a lesser extent, adults) to use suicide "attempts" to gain attention is not new. As Finch and Poznanski pointed out twenty years ago, adolescents report some 120 suicide "attempts" for every completion; adults eight for one.[32] It is evident that the vast majority of what are called "suicide attempts" are not true efforts to die, but to use the attention-grabbing drama of attempted suicide to gain some other goal.

Statistics of the past are not reliably comparable to those of the present. Suicide certification . . . requires complex investigation, dependent upon coroner technique, training, and attitude.

Similarly, the alleged contagiousness of teen suicide—whereby one suicide initiates "copycat" suicides—is rarely put in perspective appropriate to the panic raised in communities where a teen suicide has occurred. Columbia and Emory University researchers analyzed teen suicide "contagion" in 1988 and found that "cluster suicides account for approximately 1–5 percent of all teenage suicides."[33] Suicide contagion merits concern and response, but not the level of fear raised in the media and by psychological experts, which has, in any case, done nothing tangible to reduce the chances of imitators.

The myths of the generic nature of teen suicide are reflected in the well-meaning, and widely circulated, list of traits suicidal adolescents supposedly display. These include giving away prized possessions, engaging in violent arguments, remaining depressed over a period of time, suddenly changing eating or sleeping patterns, talking about death, abusing drugs or alcohol, or threatening suicide. These traits are easy to list but hard to pin down in practice, as they show up at various times in millions of individuals. It is important to understand that profiles of suicidal individuals are "unfortunately nonspecific and . . . weak," with "little empirical consensus" showing their validity in predicting suicide.[34] Non-suicidal teens (and suicidal and non-suicidal adults) also display many of these same behaviors, and more than a few teens have been shipped off to treatment based on over-reliance on such profiles.

Despite correlations so consistent they can only be called overwhelming, links between youth and adult suicide are rarely mentioned in the scientific literature and never in media treatments of the "epidemic."

Prevention programs aimed at teen suicide have shown little effectiveness.[35] Some argue, though not convincingly, that prevention efforts may actually increase teen suicide.[36] The sixfold increase in teenage psychiatric hospitalizations since 1970 cannot be shown to have reduced teen suicide either on a societal level or among the individuals in question. The failure of current efforts can be tied directly to the attempt to single out teen suicide for special attention rather than recognizing the pivotal links between general and specific adolescent and adult suicide patterns.

Beyond teen suicide myths

A couple of years ago I had an eye-opening conversation during a long bus ride with a 19-year-old West Texas rancher's daughter whose unhappy home life (mother divorced five times, molested by mom's "boyfriends" and a policeman) had led her to seriously contemplate killing herself. This young woman's searing real-life experiences contrasted starkly with the popular hype on how movies and rock 'n' roll songs cause teen suicide. Of the four Montana teen suicides I'd reported on, friends told me two had listened to classical music and jazz, one to Top-40 rock, and the fourth idolized the saccharine "Lean on Me," which is distinctly not about killing oneself. I asked this young woman if she had a favorite song that made her think of suicide. She replied, yes: "Fade to Black." Red flag. The very Metallica song singled out by Tipper's Parents Music Resource Center for promoting kids' self-dispatch. Maybe I had a case right here, if you overlook (as the PMRC does) minor details such as a childhood of rape, molestation, and parental anarchy. "I wouldn't go so far as to say that song saved my life," she said, "but hearing someone felt the way I did made me feel a lot better."

Parents can sue Judas Priest for marketing albums they claim "caused" teenage suicides, insisting that four-minute rock songs are more important than their kids' backgrounds of beatings and abandonment by alcohol-abusing parents, and win accolades and mass media attention. But youths do not kill themselves because of rock songs. There is, in reality, no such distinct phenomenon as "teen suicide." Its only distinguishing characteristic is that it is significantly lower than suicide among adults. In all other respects, it is as tragic and baffling as suicide among apparently healthy grownups.

If 500,000 teens attempt suicide annually, and only 2,000 succeed, this represents an astonishing failure rate of 250 to one.

As we have seen, teenagers commit suicide in the same patterns, by the same methods, and under the same circumstances as adults of their gender, era, and socioeconomic background. In particular, a startling and unpublicized "counter trend"—the large and unique decline in suicide among coastal California teenagers and adults over the last 25 years—is discussed in the concluding chapter.

Despite its dubious origin, the myth of the teen suicide "epidemic" is an essential argument in convincing parents that families are unable to cope with the self-destructiveness of today's youth. An American Psychological Association task force notes that claims of rising teen suicide are persuasive in winning increased commitments of marginally troubled youth to expensive psychiatric treatment.

Notes

1. Centers for Disease Control (1991, 20 September). Attempted suicide among high school students—United States, 1990. *Morbidity and Mortality Weekly Report* 40, 633–635.

2. National Center for Health Statistics (1990 and previous annual), General Mortality, Table 1-25 (Deaths from 282 selected causes by 5-year age groups, race, and sex, United States, supplementary classification of external causes of injury and poisoning). Figures on suicide by age, sex, race, and time period are from the tables in *Vital statistics of the United States* (1937– 1990), Vol II, Part A, Mortality, Table 1-25 (and previous annual); and its predecessor volume by the U.S. Bureau of the Census, *Mortality Statistics* (1900–1936).

3. Bayatpour M, Wells RD, Holford S (1992). Physical and sexual abuse as predictors of substance use and suicide among pregnant teenagers. *Journal of Adolescent Health* 13, 128–132.

4. Shogren E (1993, 20 October). Survey of top students reveals sex assaults, suicide attempts. *The Los Angeles Times*, p A22.

5. National Victim Center (1992, 23 April). *Rape in America*. Arlington, VA: NVC, Table 7.

6. See Dooley D et al (1989, Winter). Economic stress and suicide: Multilevel

analysis. *Suicide & Life-Threatening Behavior* 19, 321; Stanley M, Stanley B (1989, Spring). Biochemical studies in suicide victims: Current findings and future implications. *Suicide & Life-Threatening Behavior* 19, 30; Green A (1978). Self-destructive behavior in battered children. *American Journal of Psychiatry* 13, 579–582.

7. Freiberg P (1991, March). Sullivan is criticized by APA over report. *APA Monitor.*

8. National Center for Health Statistics (1995). *Vital statistics of the United States* 1991. Mortality, Part B. Washington, DC: U.S. Department of Health and Human Services, Table 8-5.

9. Associated Press (1995, 21 April). Child suicide rate on rise, CDC reports. Atlanta, GA.

10. U.S. Bureau of the Census (1915). *Mortality statistics.* Washington, DC: U.S. Department of Commerce, Table 7.

11. Terman L (1913, January). The tragedies of childhood. *The Forum* 49, pp 41–47.

12. Editors (1921, 23 July). Appalling rate of child suicide. *Literary Digest* 70, p 29.

13. Editors (1920, 28 August). Child suicide increasing. *Literary Digest* 66, p 23.

14. *Ibid.*

15. Terman L (1913), *op cit.*

16. *Literary Digest* (1920, 28 August), *op cit.*

17. See Adolescent suicide. *Hygeia* (1928, March), pp 125–127. The death's head on campus. *Literary Digest* (1927, 5 March), p 30.

18. Beeley AL (1932, July). Was there a suicide "wave" among college students in 1927? *Scientific Monthly* 35, pp 66–67.

19. *Science News Letter* 31 (1937, 19 June), p 392.

20. Davis PA (1983). *Suicidal adolescents.* Springfield, IL: Charles C Thomas, p 11.

21. Holinger P (1978). Adolescent suicide: An epidemiological study of recent trends. *American Journal of Psychiatry*, 135, 754–756.

22. Gist R, Welch QB (1989). Certification change versus actual behavior change in teenage suicide rates, 1955–1979. *Suicide & Life-Threatening Behavior* 19, 277–287.

23. Males M (1991, Fall). Teen suicide and changing cause-of-death certification, 1953–1987. *Suicide & Life-Threatening Behavior* 21, 245–259.

24. The correlation between teenage (age 15–19) and adult (age 20–44) suicide/self-inflicted-death trends over the 35 year period is .96 (34 df, p < .0001), indicating that 90 percent of the trends in suicidal deaths among adolescents are explained by the same factors governing such deaths among grownups.

25. Task Force on Youth Suicide (1989, January). *Report of the Secretary's Task Force on Youth Suicide.* Washington, DC: U.S. Department of Health and Human Services, pp 1, 5.

26. Kleck G (1988). Miscounting suicides. *Suicide & Life-Threatening Behavior* 18, 219–235.

27. Centers for Disease Control (1986). *Youth suicide surveillance.* Washington, DC: U.S. Department of Health and Human Services, p 1.

28. Pfeffer CR (1981, Spring). Parental suicide: An organizing event in the development of latency-age children. *Suicide & Life-Threatening Behavior,* pp 13, 43.

29. See Elkind D (1989, January). The facts about teen suicide. *Parents,* p 111. See also Associated Press (1991, 2 April) dispatch on the Gallup Survey on teen suicide, quoting experts that "5,000 to 6,000 teenagers" commit suicide annually. I sent copies of vital statistics reports to AP national editors showing this figure was 2.5 to three times too high and received acknowledgement that in the future figures would be carefully checked. They have not been.

30. CDC (1991, 20 September), *op cit,* Table 1.

31. Males M (1987, 5 April). Teen's suicide raises hard questions for Livingston youths and parents. *Bozeman Daily Chronicle,* pp 1, 2.

32. Finch SM, Pomanski EO (1971). *Adolescent suicide.* Springfield, IL: Charles C Thomas, p ix.

33. Gould MS (1989, Spring). Suicide clusters: A critical review. *Suicide & Life-Threatening Behavior,* pp 19, 25.

34. Lawrence MT, Ureda JR (1990, Summer). Student recognition of and response to suicidal peers. *Suicide & Life-Threatening Behavior* 20,164–167.

35. Hendin H (1982). *Suicide in America.* New York: WW Norton & Co., pp 182–87.

36. See Shaffer D et al (1990, 26 December). Adolescent suicide attempters, response to suicide prevention programs. *Journal of the American Medical Association* 264, 3151–3155.

11

The Extent of Homosexual Teen Suicide Is Exaggerated

Delia M. Rios

Delia M. Rios covers gender and sexuality issues for Newhouse News Service.

A study that found that gay teens are more likely than straight teens to commit suicide is flawed. The study did not establish standards for what constitutes homosexual behavior, what constitutes a suicide attempt, nor did it verify whether the teens' suicide attempts actually occurred. The fact that some gay teens are troubled should not overshadow the fact that the vast majority of teens—both gay and straight—do not kill themselves.

In a study published [in May 1998] in the journal *Pediatrics* and repeated in daily newspapers, gay teens were "more than three times as likely" to have reported a suicide attempt than heterosexual peers. But the study, as even its lead author admits, has weaknesses that are prompting others to cast doubt on this dramatic finding.

Flawed methods, flawed conclusions

Researchers have tried before to link suicide and sexual orientation but flawed methods were found to have led to flawed conclusions. Nevertheless, those flaws did not prevent dubious statistics from making their way into both public consciousness and public policy. One widely quoted and misleading statistic, in fact, was cited by Massachusetts in the creation of a Commission on Gay and Lesbian Youth.

The primary weakness of this new study, as with the ones before it, is that there is no general agreement on what constitutes a suicide attempt. In the case of the teens surveyed for this study, it was left to them to define what it meant. This study also relies on self-reporting, so there was no independent verification that suicide attempts occurred. And the "validity and reliability" of the question on sexual orientation is unclear, as the authors admit, so that the population studied may not accurately reflect

Reprinted from "Researchers Dispute Study on Gay Teens Suicide," by Delia M. Rios, *The* (New Orleans) *Times-Picayune*, May 17, 1998. Reprinted with permission from the author and the New House News Service.

the true population of gay, lesbian and bisexual students in the survey.

Pediatrician Rob Garofalo, the new study's lead author, argues that previous studies—however flawed—have been consistent with what his study shows and, weaknesses aside, he stands by his work.

"I don't agree that (the weaknesses) invalidate the study," he said.

But Garofalo, who works with troubled youths, both heterosexual and homosexual, said, "I would like to get people to stop talking about statistical risks. My studies and previous studies show issues that have been long suspected by clinicians. We know that these kids are at increased risk.

"The question is, what are we going to do about it?"

That has been the rallying cry of advocates for gay teens for years, bolstered by any number of disputed statistics from previous studies. They've used the numbers to further their own campaigns to provide gay teens with social services and school programs designed to counter a variety of ills from physical attacks by schoolmates to depression. These are all factors, they and some researchers have argued, that might ultimately lead a gay teen to a suicide attempt. Even actress Ellen DeGeneres, in a television interview, claimed that her "coming out" in her sitcom was, in part, to bolster the psyches of gay teens who might be driven to suicide.

But does the fact that there are some gay teens who are troubled necessarily mean that they are more likely to be troubled than heterosexual teens? Or that those difficulties necessarily imply a risk for suicide?

As dramatic suicide risk statistics are quoted, they obscure the fact that the vast majority of homosexual teens—and heterosexual teens—do not kill themselves. There are, overall, 5,000 adolescent suicides in the United States every year.

"Most gay kids grow up healthy, that's something I want to stress," agrees Garofalo of Children's Hospital in Boston, which is affiliated with Harvard Medical School.

Researchers have tried before to link suicide and sexual orientation but flawed methods were found to have led to flawed conclusions.

But he is equally sure that there is a "subset" of gay teens who are at risk for a range of problems from drug abuse to depression.

"I think why people have looked at this issue so much in the past is that people want to discount that these kids may be at risk of suicide attempts," Garofalo said.

The discussions revolving around gay teens and suicide have been so contentious within the research community that a conference was convened [in 1994] to address the alleged link between suicide and sexual orientation. In the end, representatives of the Centers for Disease Control, the National Institute of Mental Health, the American Psychological Association, the American Association of Suicidology, and gay and lesbian advocacy and service groups dispelled any notion of a direct or indirect link.

It simply had not been proven.

Peter Muehrer, as chief of the Youth Mental Health program of the

National Institute of Mental Health, evaluated previous studies for that conference. And nothing in what he has read in this new study—despite the authors' assertions that it breaks new ground—persuades him now that a link between gay teens and suicide has been shown.

"This just doesn't disappear," Muehrer said.

Quantifying just how many gay teens may be so troubled that they would consider killing themselves—and then comparing them with the general population—is a daunting and, as the editor of *Pediatrics* acknowledges, perhaps impossible project. There are numerous scientific obstacles, for one. And there are perhaps, editor Dr. Jerold Lucey said, too many interested viewpoints to satisfy. Statistics on the subject of gay teens and suicide, for instance, have been used by both advocates and critics of gay issues.

The defense voiced time and again when these studies come into question gives pause for science and for public policy.

"In common sense, do you think this group of children does not have an increase in suicide attempts?" Lucey asked. "Anyone who knows anything about children and adolescents knows this is a troubled group."

But the critical question remains:

How do we know?

Are personal observations good enough to qualify as science? Are they enough to determine public policy?

The scientific obstacles in proving the assertion that gay teens are more at risk for suicide attempts, Muehrer said, have yet to be overcome.

Defining the terms

There is no general agreement on how to define an attempted suicide—is it merely a suicidal thought, a half-hearted attempt, or one that requires medical attention or is actually life-threatening? Also unclear is whether suicide attempts and completed suicides are related or separate phenomena.

Then there are the difficulties in defining the term "sexual orientation." And there are also inherent weaknesses in relying on anonymous, self-reporting surveys where researchers must take a respondent's answer at face value.

As it is, the inability to define what constitutes an attempted suicide would seem to hamper any research inquiries into how often anyone tries to kill themselves.

"Because the term 'attempted suicide' potentially means so many different things, it runs the risk of meaning almost nothing at all," concluded a 1996 article in the journal of the American Association of Suicidology.

Even the new study authors noted the difficulty of their research.

"Unfortunately," they wrote, "previous research designed to examine the risks and needs of (gay, lesbian and bisexual) youth is often hampered by societal stigmas about homosexuality and difficulties identifying a representative sample population."

Their work is different, the study authors argued, because it was based on a "representative, school-based sample of adolescents."

Their research was culled from a survey of 4,159 Massachusetts ninth- to 12th-grade students. The questions on sexual orientation and suicide were part of the Centers for Disease Control and Prevention 1995 Youth

Risk Behavior Survey. Using this survey data, researchers found that 2.5 percent of the students identified themselves as gay, lesbian or bisexual. Researchers then compared "health risk behavior" between teens who identified themselves as gay, lesbian or bisexual and their heterosexual counterparts.

As dramatic suicide risk statistics are quoted, they obscure the fact that the vast majority of homosexual teens—and heterosexual teens—do not kill themselves.

In addition to increased risk for suicide, the authors claim the data shows that gay teens were more likely to have been "victimized and threatened and to have been engaged in a variety of risk behaviors," including "multiple substance use, and sexual risk behaviors."

Prompted by these findings, the study authors say gay, lesbian and bisexual teens may need "intervention efforts" as children and adolescents to stave off a host of risky behaviors, including a propensity for suicide.

In the introduction to their report, the authors cite earlier studies to support their contention that "gay, lesbian and bisexual adolescents face tremendous challenges growing up physically and mentally healthy in a culture that is often unaccepting."

One of those "studies" was a widely misrepresented report from a 1989 Task Force report on Youth Suicide by the U.S. Department of Health and Human Services. A licensed clinical social worker in San Francisco authored the report and wrote that, based on his review of existing research, gay teens were "two to three times more likely" to attempt suicide. He went further, projecting that that might also mean that 30 percent of teen suicides were by gay teens.

Although it was not based on any original research—and the research it was based on was criticized for being decades-old, non-representative and otherwise problematic—these "facts" are still in public circulation. Garofalo, author of the new study, says they were included with his work only to provide background and was not an affirmation of the study.

Garofalo, while agreeing with some of Muehrer's misgivings, said this new study at least advances research on the topic by providing information taken from a representative sample—and not, as previously done, from among groups of already troubled gay teens.

12

The Research Linking Teen Suicide and Gun Availability Is Flawed

David B. Kopel

David B. Kopel, a law professor at New York University, is the author of many articles and books on gun control, including The Samurai, the Mountie, and the Cowboy: Should America Adopt the Gun Controls of Other Democracies, *and* Guns: Who Should Have Them?

Statistics linking teen suicides with the availability of guns are blatantly in error. The number of teen suicides began to rise before guns were easily available, and furthermore, the percentage of teen suicides in which guns were used has remained stable for decades. Evidence from other countries with strict gun control laws proves that restricting guns will not reduce the number of teen suicides.

"Teen-agers in homes with guns are 75 times more likely to kill themselves than teenagers living in homes without guns," claims *Washington Post* columnist Richard Reeves. The figure has no basis in fact, and has been disavowed by its original source; but it does have an interesting genesis, which illustrates how readily factoids blossom in the gun control debate, and how they can survive even repudiation by their creators.

The *JAMA* study

In an article for the *Journal of the American Medical Association,* a pair of authors studied western Pennsylvania homes where there had been a teenage suicide, an attempted teenage suicide, or a non-suicidal teenager who had been admitted to a psychiatric hospital. A home with a teenager who had committed suicide was twice as likely to contain a gun as was a home where a teenager had attempted suicide or where a teenager with a psychiatric problem lived. The study did not analyze any homes where teenagers without psychiatric/suicide problems lived.

Nothing in the study had analyzed normal teenagers, or the risks associated with gun availability to non-mentally-ill teenagers. In an editor-

Excerpted from "Children and Guns: Sensible Solutions," by David B. Kopel, available at www.shadeslanding.com/firearms/children.guns.html, April 25, 1993. Reprinted with permission from the author.

ial accompanying the article, three employees of the federal Centers for Disease Control wrote: "the odds that potential suicidal adolescents will kill themselves go up 75-fold when a gun is kept in the home." But nothing in the article supported a "75-fold" claim. In fact, the article suggested that the risk could increase more than two-fold. The *Journal* later published a retraction stating that instead of "75-fold," the editorial should have said "more than double." And in any case, the data did not reveal anything about normal teenagers.

Unfortunately, anti-gun advocates who noticed the incorrect "75-fold" claim do not appear to have noticed the *Journal*'s correction. Senator John Chafee (R-RI), the prime sponsor of a bill to confiscate all handguns, repeated the "75-fold" figure to a Congressional committee. And columnist Reeves took the figure one step further, by telling his readers that the "75-fold" figure applies to all teenagers, rather than only to the severely troubled teenagers that the *Journal* article had studied. Over ninety percent of persons who commit suicide have a psychiatric illness at the time of their act.

The rise in teenage suicide began before handgun availability began to rise sharply.

Yet while suicides are usually committed by persons with mental illnesses, it is also true that a large percentage of adolescents report planning a suicide (19%), and a significant percentage claim to have actually attempted suicide (7%). Accordingly, cautious parents of teenagers may well choose to keep their guns locked and disassembled, even if their teenagers do not suffer from mental illness. But is the research evidence about suicide strong enough for legislatures to turn every parent who has a teenager and a handgun in the same home into a criminal? Or to force every gun be locked up, regardless of the particular families' circumstances? A careful review of the evidence suggests not.

An illogical conclusion

First of all, gun prohibition advocates' leap from data regarding mentally ill teenagers to conclusions about teenagers as a whole is illogical. By analogy, it is likely true that convicted felons who own cars are more likely to commit bank robberies than those who have less access to ready means of escape. Such a finding would demonstrate that cars facilitate robbery (as guns can facilitate suicide). The car and robbery information might suggest prophylactic legislation such as cross-referencing automobile ownership and felony records, or even restrictions on felons owning cars. But the information would not suggest that any such law would have a significant impact in reducing robbery, or that cars "cause" robbery, or that law-abiding citizens should be forbidden to own cars.

Senator Chafee and Mr. Reeves are not the only persons who have gotten confused about the data regarding teenage gun suicide. The American Academy of Pediatrics told a Congressional committee, "Every three hours, a teenager commits suicide with a handgun." The Educational

Fund to End Gun Violence, and Handgun Control, Inc. also repeat the "every three hours" figure, although they claim the figure is for "firearms" rather than just handguns. But the "every three hours" figure is correct only if one counts all suicides, not just gun suicides, or if one calls every person under age 25 a "teenager." The teenage gun suicide rate is only half what the anti-gun organizations contend.

Gun prohibition advocates insist that America is suffering a teenage suicide epidemic. In 1992, the American Academy of Pediatrics endorsed a handgun ban while claiming "Adolescent suicides are rising sharply, and most involve handguns."

Youth suicide rates are stable

In fact, youth suicides are not rising sharply. The youth suicide rate has been relatively stable during the 1980s and 1990s, after rising sharply in the 1960s and 1970s.

The data suggest that nothing happening in recent years regarding youth suicide should encourage hasty measures based on panic about a "sudden" crisis. As Dr. L.D. Hankoff, of the New Jersey Medical Center wrote in the *Journal of the American Medical Association:*

> While there has been a rise in youth suicide in the past two decades, the rates for ages 15 to 24 are lower than for any older age group. It is important to take the long view of what may appear as an epidemic. The suicide rate of persons 15 to 24 took a sharp rise around 1905 and dropped off sharply by 1920, and there is a suggestion that the rate in that group has begun to level off now after a peak increase. More importantly, the rush to school-based programs for youth suicide prevention has lacked an empirical base, produced no measurable benefit, and consumed precious health care resources.

During the period from the mid-1950s to the mid-1970s, when teenage suicide was rising, most of the increasing suicide rate was attributable to gun suicides. Accordingly, some physicians have contended that increasing handgun availability is associated with increased teenage suicide.

But the data do not necessarily support this conclusion. The rise in teenage suicide began before handgun availability began to rise sharply. When the rate of handgun increase was at its highest—in 1980—teenage suicide had leveled off. The percentage of guns involved in teenage suicides has remained stable since the mid-1970s.

Gun control laws have no effect on suicide

Moreover, the evidence does not support the conclusion that gun control will reduce suicide. The increase in teenage suicide with firearms that occurred in the late 1960s and the first part of the next decade occurred at the same time as the greatest increase in gun control laws in American history. Congress outlawed interstate gun sales (with a few exceptions), required that all guns be registered at the point of sale, and banned the import of cheap handguns. Sales of handguns to persons under 21 were prohibited, as were sales of any gun to persons under 18. At the same time, many states and cities enacted substantially more restrictive laws, with the laws falling most heavily on handguns, the gun used most in suicide.

Some researchers believe that removing one method of suicide can lower the overall suicide rate. Other researchers believe that removing one means will simply result in potential suicides choosing another means. One of the most famous efforts to remove a means of suicide has been the detoxification of household gas. Some researchers have found a major life-saving effect from the detoxification, while other researchers have found no impact at all.

In regards to firearms, the research becomes even more difficult, for no American community has ever completely removed firearms, the way many communities could completely remove toxic household gas. (Since household gas must be continuously supplied from a central source, gas is much easier than guns, which are privately owned.)

Florida State University criminologist Gary Kleck (a liberal Democrat and an ACLU member), analyzed gun control laws and suicide rates in every American city with a population over 100,000. Cross-tabulating the various cities to account for all the factors that might affect suicide, such as race (whites are more likely to be suicides), religion (Catholics are less likely), economic circumstances, and 19 gun control laws, ranging from waiting periods to handgun bans, Kleck found no statistically significant evidence that any of the gun control laws affected the suicide rate.

Data from other countries appear to support Kleck's conclusion that gun control is not an effective method for reducing suicide. While teenage suicide has remained stable in the U.S. in the last 15 years, teenage suicide has risen sharply in Europe, where gun control is much stricter. In Great Britain, where gun control laws are extremely severe, and the gun ownership rate is less than 1/10th of that in America, adolescent suicide has risen by more than 25% in just five years.

Similarly, Japan outlaws handguns and rifles, and makes shotguns extremely difficult to obtain. Yet teenage suicide is 30% more frequent in Japan than in America.

Perhaps one reason that gun controls do not reduce suicide is that equally lethal methods are commonly available. Hanging, carbon monoxide auto exhaust gas, and drowning are all about as likely as guns to result in a "successful" suicide.

Comparisons with Canada

Canadian gun controls are sometimes cited as having reduced suicide, although the evidence is not so clear as gun prohibitionists contend. In 1977, Canada enacted a law requiring a person wishing to buy a long gun to acquire a government license. Handguns were already subject to a fairly strict licensing system. According to a Canadian government study, suicides involving firearms dropped noticeably after 1978, reversing the previous trend. Unfortunately, the overall Canadian suicide rate increased slightly. America's suicide rate declined slightly in the same period (while American gun control laws were being relaxed).

One study in the *New England Journal of Medicine* compared the suicide rates of Seattle and Vancouver. While Seattle's handgun suicide rate was five times higher than Vancouver's, Vancouver's overall suicide was greater. The suicide rate in Vancouver was higher for all age groups except one. That one group was persons aged 15–24. In reporting the research, the authors emphasized the lower youth suicide rate in Vancouver. The authors asserted that gun control might reduce young people's suicide, even if it had no overall effect on total suicide rates.

Logically speaking, the study's assertion was untenable. The fact that Vancouver has stricter gun laws and a lower teenage suicide rate does not prove that the strict laws caused the low youth suicide rate. The error is referred to as Argument from False Cause. To say: "Vancouver has severe gun laws, and Vancouver has a lower youth suicide rate. Therefore, gun laws reduce youth suicide," is no more logical than to say: "New York City has more churches than any other American city; New York City has more crime than any other American city. Therefore, churches cause crime." It would have been just as (il)logical to say "Vancouver has strict gun laws; Vancouver has a higher suicide rate in most age groups. Therefore strict gun laws cause suicide."

The simplistic assertion that strict gun control somehow lowered the Vancouver youth suicide, while having no responsibility for the higher suicide rates in other age groups, was hardly persuasive. The assertion about the benefit of Vancouver's stricter laws was further undermined by the fact that at the time of the study, gun controls in Canada for teenagers were actually less formally restrictive than American laws for teenagers.

Although the *New England Journal* article received extensive media publicity, another study which came out the same year was little noticed outside of scholarly circles. That study analyzed suicide rates in Toronto and San Diego.

The difficult topic of teenage suicide is made even more difficult by the introduction of erroneous statistics and sloppy research.

The Toronto portion of the study found that the 1977 Canadian gun laws had decreased firearms suicide by men. The San Diego portion of the study looked only at mental patients, who are forbidden by California law to possess guns, and also found that the law reduces firearms suicide by men. (The firearms suicide rate for women was already low.) But while firearms suicide in Toronto and San Diego declined, suicide did not. "[T]he difference was apparently offset by an increase in suicide by leaping."

The Canadian data are consistent with American data, which show that areas with fewer guns do have fewer gun suicides—but they do not have overall lower suicide rates.

In sum, the assertion that gun control is a sure method of reducing teenage suicide is not nearly as certain as the gun prohibition lobbies insist. Too often, the difficult topic of teenage suicide is made even more difficult by the introduction of erroneous statistics and sloppy research.

13

Heavy Metal Music Does Not Contribute to Teen Suicide

T. Galas-Gray

T. Galas-Gray is a Canadian representative of the international organization Portrait of an American Family Association, a group that battles censorship of the heavy metal group Marilyn Manson.

Many teens listen to heavy metal music because the lyrics mirror their feelings of anger, alienation, depression, and rebelliousness. Heavy metal music lets these teens know they are not alone with their problems. The idea that listening to heavy metal music causes teens to commit suicide is ludicrous. People who commit suicide do so for reasons unrelated to the music they listen to. People must stop blaming music for causing life's problems.

Can music kill? This is a question that just won't go away. First it was Ozzy in the 70's and then Metallica in the 80's. Now in the 90's the conservative right is using the band Marilyn Manson as their latest target of blame. Yet just as many times as this question has been posed, it has also been shot down in the courts through dismissal or being thrown out. The fact of the matter is, music is not the cause. It is, however, something to relate to, and, yes, at times, a symptom of how an adolescent or listener of any age may be feeling. The operative word here is feeling. Too often, parents forget what this time of life is like. Isolation, loneliness, feeling like no one understands you, feeling like you are the only one who feels that way or has those problems—these are dilemmas faced all too often by adolescents today, possibly even more so than in years past. It is a time of wanting to fit in, sometimes desperately so. And it is a time of trying to answer the question "Just who am I anyway?"

Therefore, is it really so surprising that increasingly more adolescents suffer from depression and/or choose to take their own lives? This is a generation that has been raised by TV and other forms of media that imply that in order to fit in you have to look, act, be a certain way. And if

Reprinted from "Suicide and Music: Can Music Kill?" by T. Galas-Gray, available at www. spookykids.marilyn.manson.com. Reprinted with permission from the author.

you don't? Well, then you're not cool, you're not good enough. And this does not just affect women. The fact that eating disorders in males are on the rise is proof of this. Furthermore, with a divorce rate of nearly 50 percent, many teens come from broken and dysfunctional families. And even traditional nuclear families that remain intact are not immune to being dysfunctional.

The sad truth of the matter is many kids today feel like they can't talk to their parents for fear they will either get angry, fail to understand or not really *HEAR* what they are saying/feeling. It is for this reason, many teens turn to music and their peers for support. While one might assume listening to "happy-go-lucky" music would make a troubled or depressed youth feel better, the reality is often quite the opposite because they can relate much more to music that mirrors how they are feeling. From this perspective, it is not at all surprising that so many young people listen to music that their parents consider rebellious, depressing or angry. Yet more often than not, these individuals get through it. The MUSIC helps them get through it, in many cases giving them a sense of joy only a true music lover can comprehend and a sense of not being alone. Additionally, most of these individuals grow up to be healthy, productive members of society, despite their troubled adolescence and the equally angst-ridden music they may listen to.

But what about the ones who do not fare so well? The question of this was recently propelled back into the spotlight when Raymond Kuntz testified before the US Congress that he believed Marilyn Manson's music caused his son Richard to end his life. Once again, we come to the issue of rock music being a target, a scapegoat. While it would be inhuman not to sympathize with this man's grief, it is painfully obvious he, along with many other grieving parents, is looking for something to blame. After all, it is human nature. People like to have a sense of control over things, and when tragic things happen, especially to loved ones, people instinctively look for something or someone to blame. And, with all the recent controversy Marilyn Manson has received, who better a target? Certainly it is much more palatable for Mr. Kuntz to blame Marilyn Manson than to acknowledge the possibility maybe, just maybe, he wasn't the perfect parent, wasn't everything his son needed or just simply didn't see the warning signs that were right in front of him.

Thousands of people of many ages listen to the music of bands like Marilyn Manson, yet only a select few choose suicide.

And how convenient it is that several other details of the case were overlooked. For instance, the boy's best friend had killed himself a month or two prior to Richard's death, so obviously he would be grieving and depressed over this loss. Why is it Marilyn Manson was blamed for this child's death? It is pretty simple, really. Blaming Marilyn Manson is easier than taking a long, hard sobering look at what was really going on in that child's life. Mr. Kuntz claimed that his son was a normal kid in every way and it was Marilyn Manson's music and lyrics that made his son kill himself. Yet, how can he say his son was fine when he had just lost a close friend to suicide? Denial is clearly at work here.

Furthermore, it should be noted that in countless interviews, Marilyn Manson has stated the following to fans and the media:

1. It is STUPID and WEAK to kill yourself.
2. You should persevere and believe in yourself even when no one else will.
3. He is saddened that people would be so stupid as to kill themselves, be it over a song or anything else.

It should also be noted that many fans of this band have stated that Manson's music actually HELPS them to be strong, to stick with life and not give up. And in some cases, Marilyn Manson's message of individual strength has helped inspire some fans from committing suicide.

Copycat suicides

However, Richard and his friend committing suicide so close to each other time-wise does bring up the issue of copycat suicide, a phenomenon often mistaken for being a result of the music these kids listen to and imaginary teen cults that in fact only exist in the minds of these uninformed people. What they fail to realize is it is not uncommon for one suicide, especially when highly publicized, to lead to future suicides. Copycat suicides have been documented time and time again, and are possibly even more common than research has been able to show. Often the news of a friend or classmate having killed themselves is just the push an already troubled youth needs to be sent over the edge and follow in their departed classmate's footsteps. And when it is a best friend, the risk increases.

As was stated above, adolescence is a time when teens will turn to their friends and music for support. When one of those support systems is suddenly shattered by the suicide of a friend, or even an accidental death, thoughts of taking one's own life aren't uncommon to youths who already feel alone or like that was the only friend they could really count on. Even the suicide of a distant acquaintance has been shown to result in copycat suicides. For instance, research I have read suggests that the rate of plane crashes following a supposedly accidental crash increases 100 fold in the area where the crash is publicized. It is thought that these are in fact copycat suicides, rather than accidents.

Additionally, research has shown that individuals who take their own lives, or attempt to, would have done so regardless of who their favourite rock band is. Research also suggests that such individuals often had suicidal thoughts prior to learning of a classmate's suicide. And if youth misinterpret the music of a band in such a way that they actually take their own lives *because* they think that is what the music is telling them to do, they clearly had problems long before the music ever came along. It is unfair and simple-minded to blame an artist for misinterpretations of their work, especially when they have stated in numerous interviews what they intended the message of their work to be.

In reality, thousands of people of many ages listen to the music of bands like Marilyn Manson, yet only a select few choose suicide. There are probably equally as many Spice Girls fans who take their own lives or kill themselves through anorexia, yet are the Spice Girls blamed for this? Of course not. It is much easier to blame bands like Marilyn Manson who portray society's problems realistically, than the Spice Girls, whose lyrics are all about perfect romances, joy, and how good life is. Yet life is not all sugar and spice, and anyone who believes it is is in for a serious disappointment. Without a doubt, many adolescent girls—who listen to these happy songs and look at these women in their skimpy dresses—compare themselves to what they see and hear and find they do not measure up. Yet, blaming the Spice Girls for adolescent anorexia is just as ludicrous as blaming Marilyn Manson for teen suicide.

Life is much more complex, and until parents and others who deal with youth realize that and stop blaming music for problems that go much deeper, this problem will only get worse. The fact that two of five suicides in Sudbury, Ontario, Canada, have been blamed yet again on Marilyn Manson (and the band's T-shirts subsequently banned in a Sudbury high school) is proof people still fail to grasp this crucial point. Scapegoating doesn't heal the wounds, it only covers them, leaving them to fester below the surface while the real problem continues to be ignored.

Organizations to Contact

The editors have compiled the following list of organizations concerned with the issues debated in this book. The descriptions are derived from materials provided by the organizations. All have publications or information available for interested readers. The list was compiled on the date of publication of the present volume; the information provided here may change. Be aware that many organizations take several weeks or longer to respond to inquiries, so allow as much time as possible.

American Association of Suicidology (AAS)

4201 Connecticut Ave. NW, Suite 408, Washington, DC 20008
(202) 237-2280 • fax: (202) 237-2282
e-mail: debbiehu@ix.netcom.com • website: http://www.suicidology.org

The association is one of the largest suicide prevention organizations in the United States. It promotes the view that suicidal thoughts are almost always a symptom of depression and that suicide is almost never a rational decision. In addition to prevention of suicide, the group also works to increase public awareness about suicide and to help those grieving the death of a loved one to suicide. The association publishes the quarterly newsletters *American Association of Suicidology—Newslink* and *Surviving Suicide*, and the quarterly journal *Suicide and Life Threatening Behavior.*

American Foundation for Suicide Prevention (AFSP)

120 Wall Street, 22nd Floor, New York, NY 10005
(888) 333-2377 • fax: (212) 363-6237
e-mail: rfabrika@afsp.org • website: http://www.afsp.org

Formerly known as the American Suicide Foundation, the AFSP supports scientific research on depression and suicide, educates the public and professionals on the recognition and treatment of depressed and suicidal individuals, and provides support programs for those coping with the loss of a loved one to suicide. AFSP publishes the newsletter *Crisis* and the quarterly *Lifesavers.*

American Psychiatric Association

1400 K St. NW, Washington, DC 20005
(202) 682-6000 • fax: (202) 682-6850
e-mail: apa@psych.org • website: http://www.psych.org

An organization of psychiatrists dedicated to studying the nature, treatment, and prevention of mental disorders, the APA helps create mental health policies, distributes information about psychiatry, and promotes psychiatric research and education. It publishes the *American Journal of Psychiatry* and *Psychiatric News* monthly.

American Psychological Association (APA)

750 First St. NE, Washington DC 20002-4242
(202) 336-5500 • fax: (202) 336-5708
e-mail: public.affairs@apa.org • web address: http://www.apa.org

This professional organization for psychologists aims to "advance psychology as a science, as a profession, and as a means of promoting human welfare." It produces numerous publications, including the book *Adolescent Suicide: Assessment and Intervention*, the report "Researcher Links Perfectionism in High Achievers with Depression and Suicide," and the online guide *Warning Signs—A Violence Prevention Guide for Youth*.

Canadian Association for Suicide Prevention (CASP)
#301, 11456 Jasper Ave. NW, Edmonton, Alberta, T5K 0M1 Canada
(780) 482-0198 • fax: (780) 488-1495
e-mail: casp@suicideprevention.ca
website: http://www.compusmart.ab.ca/supnet/casp.htm

CASP organizes annual conferences and educational programs on suicide prevention. It publishes the newsletter *CASP News* three times a year and the booklet *Suicide Prevention in Canadian Schools*.

Depression and Related Affective Disorders Association (DRADA)
Meyer 3-181, 600 N. Wolfe St., Baltimore, MD 21287-7381
(410) 955-4647
e-mail: drada@jhmi.edu • website: http://www.med.jhu.edu/drada

DRADA, a nonprofit organization that works in cooperation with the Department of Psychiatry at the Johns Hopkins University School of Medicine, seeks to alleviate the suffering arising from depression and manic depression by assisting self-help groups, providing education and information, and lending support to research programs. It publishes the report "A Look at . . . Suicide, a Relentless and Underrated Foe" and the book *Night Falls Fast—Understanding Suicide*.

Foundation of Thanatology
630 W. 168th St., New York, NY 10032
(212) 928-2066 • fax: (718) 549-7219

This organization of health, theology, psychology, and social science professionals is devoted to scientific and humanist inquiries into health, loss, grief, and bereavement. The foundation coordinates professional, educational, and research programs concerned with mortality and grief. It publishes the periodicals *Advances in Thanatology* and *Archives of the Foundation of Thanatology*.

National Alliance for the Mentally Ill (NAMI)
200 N. Glebe Rd., Suite 1015, Arlington, VA 22203-3754
(800) 950-6264 • fax: (703) 524-9094
website: http://www.nami.org

NAMI is a consumer advocacy and support organization composed largely of family members of people with severe mental illnesses such as schizophrenia, manic-depressive illness, and depression. The alliance adheres to the position that severe mental illnesses are biological brain diseases and that mentally ill people should not be blamed or stigmatized for their conditions. NAMI favors increased government funding for research, treatment, and community services for the mentally ill. Its publications include the bimonthly newsletter *NAMI Advocate*, as well as various brochures, handbooks, and policy recommendations.

National Depressive and Manic-Depressive Association (NDMDA)
730 N. Franklin St., Suite 501, Chicago, IL 60610-3526
(800) 826-3632 • (312) 642-0049 • fax: (312) 642-7243
e-mail: arobinson@ndmda.org • website: http://www.ndmda.org

The association provides support and advocacy for patients with depression and manic-depressive illness. It seeks to persuade the public that these disorders are biochemical in nature and to end the stigmatization of people who suffer from them. It publishes the quarterly *NDMDA Newsletter* and various books and pamphlets.

National Foundation for Depressive Illness (NAFDI)
PO Box 2257, New York, NY 10116
(800) 239-1265
website: http://www.depression.org

NAFDI informs the public, health care providers, and corporations about depression and manic-depressive illness. It promotes the view that these disorders are physical illnesses treatable with medication, and it believes that such medication should be made readily available to those who need it. The foundation maintains several toll-free telephone lines and distributes brochures, bibliographies, and literature on the symptoms of and treatments for depression and manic-depressive illness. It also publishes the quarterly newsletter *NAFDI News.*

Samaritans
10 The Grove, Slough, Berkshire SL1 1QP UK
01753 216500 • fax: 01753 775787
e-mail: jo@samaritans.org • website: http://www.samaritans.org.uk

Samaritans is the largest suicide prevention organization in the world. Established in England in 1953, the organization now has branches in at least forty-four nations throughout the world. The group's volunteers provide counseling and other assistance to suicidal and despondent individuals. In addition, Samaritans publishes the booklets *Teen Suicide Information and Guidelines for Parents* and *The Suicidal Student: A Guide for Educators.*

SA\VE—Suicide Awareness\Voices of Education
PO Box 24507, Minneapolis, MN 55424-0507
(612) 946-7998
e-mail: save@winternet.com • website: http://www.save.org

SA\VE works to prevent suicide and to help those grieving after the suicide of a loved one. Its members believe that brain diseases, such as depression, should be detected and treated promptly because they can result in suicide. In addition to pamphlets and the book *Suicide: Survivors—A Guide for Those Left Behind*, the organization publishes the quarterly newsletter *Voices.*

Suicide Information and Education Centre (SIEC)
#201, 1615 10th Ave. SW, Calgary, Alberta T3C 0J7 Canada
(403) 245-3900 • fax: (403) 245-0299
e-mail: siec@siec.ca • website: http://www.siec.ca

The Suicide Information and Education Centre acquires and distributes information on suicide prevention. It maintains a computerized database, a free mailing list, and a document delivery service. It publishes the quarterly *Current Awareness Bulletin* and the monthly *SIEC Clipping Service.*

Bibliography

Books

Leroy Aarons — *Prayers for Bobby: A Mother's Coming to Terms with the Suicide of Her Gay Son*. San Francisco: HarperSanFrancisco, 1995.

Jillayne Arena — *Step Back from the Exit: 45 Reasons to Say No to Suicide*. Milwaukee, WI: Zebulon Press, 1996.

Alan L. Berman and David A. Jobes — *Adolescent Suicide: Assessment and Intervention*. Washington, DC: American Psychological Association, 1996.

Bev Cobain — *When Nothing Matters Anymore: A Survival Guide for Depressed Teens*. Minneapolis: Free Spirit, 1998.

Committee on Adolescence — *Adolescent Suicide*. Washington, DC: American Psychiatric Press, 1996.

John Donnelly, ed. — *Suicide: Right or Wrong?* 2nd ed. Amherst, NY: Prometheus Books, 1998.

Bernard Frankel and Rachel Kranz — *Straight Talk About Teenage Suicide*. New York: Facts On File, 1994.

Herbert Hendin — *Suicide in America*. New York: Norton, 1995.

Paul C. Holinger et al. — *Suicide and Homicide Among Adolescents*. New York: Guilford Press, 1994.

Susan Kuklin — *After a Suicide: Young People Speak Up*. New York: Putnam, 1994.

David Lester — *Making Sense of Suicide: An In-Depth Look at Why People Kill Themselves*. Philadelphia: Charles Press, 1997.

Robert Emmet Long — *Suicide*. New York: HW Wilson, 1995.

Eric Marcus — *Why Suicide? Answers to 200 of the Most Frequently Asked Questions About Suicide, Attempted Suicide, and Assisted Suicide*. San Francisco: HarperSanFrancisco, 1996.

Richard E. Nelson and Judith C. Galas — *The Power to Prevent Suicide: A Guide for Teens Helping Teens*. Minneapolis: Free Spirit, 1994.

Gary Remafedi, ed. — *Death by Denial: Studies of Suicide in Gay and Lesbian Teenagers*. Boston: Alyson Publications, 1994.

Ralph L.V. Rickgarn — *Perspectives on College Student Suicide*. Amityville, NY: Baywood, 1994.

Paul R. Robbins — *Adolescent Suicide*. Jefferson, NC: McFarland & Co., 1998.

Andrew E. Slaby and Lili Frank Garfinkel — *No One Saw My Pain: Why Teens Kill Themselves*. New York: Norton, 1994.

Kate Williams   *A Parent's Guide for Suicidal and Depressed Teens*. Center City, MN: Hazelden, 1995.

Periodicals

Janice Arenofsky   "Teen Suicide: When the Blues Get Out of Control," *Current Health 2*, December 1997.

Susan Bartok   "My Twin Sister Committed Suicide," *'Teen*, January 1999.

Pam Belluck   "Black Youths' Rate of Suicide Rising Sharply, Studies Find," *New York Times*, March 20, 1998.

Pam Belluck   "In Little City Safe from Violence, Rash of Suicides Leaves Scars," *New York Times*, April 5, 1998.

Brenda Branswell   "Death and 'Taxing': Did Teen Extortion Play a Role in Four Suicides?" *Maclean's*, October 13, 1997.

Rae Corelli   "Killing the Pain," *Maclean's*, January 29, 1996.

Theodore Dalrymple   "Good-bye, Cruel World," *City Journal*, Winter 1997. Available from 52 Vanderbilt Ave., New York, NY 10017.

Francesca Delbanco   "The Heart of Darkness," *Seventeen*, November 1998.

Nancy Dreher   "The Teen Years: Risky Business?" *Current Health 2*, September 1996.

Elizabeth Gleick   "Suicide's Shadow," *Time*, July 22, 1996.

Elizabeth Kaye   "To Die For," *Esquire*, May 1996.

Timothy E. Moore   "Scientific Consensus and Expert Testimony: Lessons from the Judas Priest Trial," *Skeptical Inquirer*, November/December 1996.

Patrick Perry   "Teens at Risk," *Saturday Evening Post*, January/February 1999.

Cathy A. Pohan and Norma J. Bailey   "Including Gays in Multiculturalism," *Education Digest*, January 1998.

Delia M. Rios   "A Bogus Statistic that Won't Go Away," *American Journalism Review*, July/August 1997.

Leslie Sadasivan and Cynthia Hanson   "My Son Didn't Have to Die," *Ladies Home Journal*, May 1998.

'Teen   "The Heartbreaking Reality of Suicide Pacts," August 1996.

'Teen   "I Tried to Commit Suicide Because My Boyfriend Broke Up with Me," October 1995.

Alex Tresniowski   "Song of Hope," *People*, November 30, 1998.

Catherine Walsh   "Preventing Teenage Suicide," *America*, April 12, 1997.

Andrea Young Ward   "The Question of Life," *Common Boundary*, July/August 1996. Available from PO Box 445, Mt. Morris, IL 61054.

Laura Ziv   "The Tragedy of Teen Suicide," *Sassy*, November 1996.

Index